The Tao of Prayer:

Looking East to See the Rest

©2017 Patrick Easter,

Lawrenceville, GA, USA

Table of Contents

Introduction..3
A Not So Crazy Quilt.................................6
Wisdom in Small Doses..........................11
The Living Tao..12
The Commune..56
Learning by Forgetting...........................59
From Detachment to Mastery................66
The Spirit Book.......................................72
Know Yourself..84
"We Knew Not Where We Were!"..........111
Breaking the Image..............................115
Restoring the Image.............................120
The Work of the People........................127
Contemplation......................................146
The Quiet Way......................................148
The Soul Friend....................................171
As You Have Done................................173
Beginning..180
Acknowledgments................................184
Closing notes:.......................................186
Further Reading:...................................187
And Now, the End Notes:.....................197

Introduction

I've been careful to keep this book short – weaving a small tapestry, rather than spinning a long yarn. A lot of thinking, a lot of living, and one question have gone into it. Can our bodies shape our spirits? Why do some monks sit in just such a position, or hold their hands just so? Why do some focus on their navels, or others on a spot that isn't on the wall? One stands all night in icy seawater and another's feet wear deep prints in his floor from long hours standing on the same spot. Some gain unspeakable wisdom from the voice of a running stream.

People have been doing such things for thousands of years. It must be worth something. We still do them. In fact, people who do these things are known in their generations as wise teachers. What do these motions do? Do physical movements perfect the soul? What does silence teach us? These mysteries seem to be as old as the human race. I think they're worth exploring. Do you agree? Let's walk together, then, shall we?

~§~

What is "truth?" What are the answers to the Big Questions? Is there life after death? Before death? What is life? What is death? Where do we fit into the Big Picture? How can we know? What is the best way to be, to live? What thinking person believes exactly as Confucius, Calvin, or Kant? Even these men learned, changed, and erred along the way. The reliable teacher knows the answers. The better one embodies them. The ideal is the truth, behind the truths, embodied.,

~§~

A Not So Crazy Quilt

In my grandmother's house, on her bed, was a quilt. She called it her "crazy quilt." It didn't seem to follow any certain pattern, like the Wedding Ring or the North Star. Truth is, though, it wasn't so crazy after all, as each patch had its own story: This one might be from the nightgown of her brother, who died at nine months of typhus. This other one, possibly from her own favorite dancing dress, when a teenager. That patch was from the suit jacket her father wore when he married her mother, back when a gentleman was known by his team and carriage. So, while it may not have been laid out in the splendid fashion of those on display in the National Quilt Museum, or shown for sale at an Amish fruit stand, this crazy quilt held the memories of many lives, in a form to give comfort on the coldest nights, and was held together in such a way as to say that the memories, and so the strength and the hopes of those lives would continue. This is the kind of crazy we all need a little more of. Wouldn't you agree?

Growing up is hazardous. Parents are often too busy building their own lives to help their children build theirs. Grandparents might fill that gap. They can come into our lives with the needed wisdom, in a deep bag of experience, of lessons learned. Usually learned the hard way. Yet, when they show up, we are so often too young, and too, too shortsighted to notice much else but the outward quirks, tics, and scars. Grandmama was like that. A loving and compassionate woman, yet stubborn in a way that only someone who had survived by her stubbornness could understand. Every rag, such as you or I might toss, would go to a quilt, a rug braid, or for cleaning house. Old newspapers that weren't folded into trash can liners she used to line her flower-drying boxes, and she was a Marie Curie in the science of flower preservation, her own kind of sculptor in the lost art of dried bouquets. Every aspect of her life reflected a wisdom I was not prepared to see.

Widowed in the winter of 1929 with an infant son and a three-year-old daughter, she had had little choice but to move back in with her parents. Although her father was one of the wealthiest men in that town she had to make her own way, clearing the back yard with a shuffle hoe to put in exotic plants for the florists' market. As she weathered the Depression, her frugality and her strict, Presbyterian work ethic truly became her. I was at her house almost as much as my own parents', but I was too busy being a kid, playing with loose dogs, climbing trees, and harassing cats to stop and learn about how her parents had emigrated from dear County Tyrone, or how she had worked her flower business, or what it was like living her life. I was entirely too busy muddling about with my own!

~§~

Related to us or not, we need wise soul-friends in this life – men and women who have devoted their lives to "searching and seeking out all wisdom," as the old scrolls read. These people may not have had little children underfoot to distract them, or the seducing comforts of even a soft bed at night. For these, wisdom is more than quilt patches – it is the lessons learned from them. Uncle Willy's death was tragic. Is this sadness wasted? Grandda' John's fine coat is braided into a rug. Can we learn something from this? A sage is devoted to what life really is about, damn the cost. A soul-friend understand us.

~§~

Wisdom in Small Doses

As a child I loved the old Charlie Chan movies. This mysterious detective was always making these "Confucius say..." statements that seemed to always say more than was spoken. Maybe they were clues to the mystery or just a way of making the character out to be more of an "inscrutable Chinaman" than he was. (Neither writer nor actor was the first part Chinese.) But it intrigued me when many words were spoken with only a few being said. Beyond the detective movies' pithy lines, deeper words from Confucius' *Analects*, Solomon's wisdom writings, Lao Tse's *Tao Te Ching*, and Christ's Beatitudes and parables made me look beyond appearances. The words would say one thing, but then again, what, really? There is a lot more to living than making it to the next distraction.

We talk about wisdom, truth and meaning, but what are they? We can say that real *truth* is what we have if we know all the data there is, about every atom and cell, of ever particle and fiber, of the whole fabric of the universe, every spiritual being, all science, art, and philosophy, and how every part fits the other, we would have data. If we understood our own lives and just how they relate to that whole big picture, and how we might best live our lives in that relationship, that is what I am calling "truth." Another, much older, word for this is, *Tao*.

The Living Tao

Winston Churchill once said, so they say, "Men occasionally stumble over the truth, but most of them pick themselves up, and hurry off, as if nothing ever happened."

Once in a while a good idea even crosses my mind. Most pass by unnoticed.

Once upon a time I had my own little place in "the Dream." Family, house, yard, career, a nice motorcycle, comfortable opinions, all that. What could go wrong? But what would I be, I wondered, if I didn't have these things to "show for myself?" How was I better, really, than a hermit crab? Nobody sees much of the crab but what kind of shell or can it's picked up to cover its own substantial hind end. We look into the surf and it looks like a can of tomatoes is making its way along the sand. I didn't see much reason to worry about losing my *can*, but noticed how I saw myself through all these things I had happened to pick up along the way. I had all these *in* my life, but they weren't me, and I wasn't them. Then one day I had a change of clothes, a shaving kit, and the bike. Scratch the bike. That was it. The shock was pretty unnerving, but once the dust cleared I was still me. In fact, it turned out I was better off. How? It's an ongoing thing. Life is, you know? I won't tell other people's stories, and the details won't help this story. I can, though, start a little farther back and offer a story that works for all of us, rich or homeless, single, married, or monastic. Let's pick up that story somewhere in the middle, around 2,700 years back, in fact, with a book written back then. A short book, it always gave me a feeling of being wiser than I was, from being in the conversation with the writer. It is called the *Tao Te Ching*. I hope I have learned a little since then.

Back in the middle of the sixth century BCE the Zhou emperor's court historian was Li Erh Tan. People called him, "Old Sage," or, in Chinese, *Lao Tse*.[1] He understood the way of peace; and the ways the divine energies move in this world and hold it together. It is that love this book seeks to express.

Some say he started the Taoist religion. He didn't, but his verses formed the basis for Taoist thought. The young lad Confucius, we are told, would visit him to ask questions. What bit we have of his wisdom, these 81 "verses," is called the *Tao Te Ching*.

The very title speaks volumes. *Tao* is the deepest word. It can mean Way, Word, or Universal Principle. *Te,* Power, Heart, or Virtue, as the divine virtue by which the *Tao* guides the universe[2]. *Ching* can be as simple as "Book," or as heavy as "Changeless," "Canon," or, "Law." So we *can* read it as the *Law of Principle and Virtue*.

Of course, this little book is almost 2,700 years old, and there is plenty in it that most of us will never see, living in such a different age. Scholars to this day devote their careers to this Ching, and are sure to have some things to say about it.[3]

If we know the past, we understand the future. He could see the kingdom heading into collapse with no way to stop it. This was all just too much for him.

His apartment would have been in the palace compound. Out beyond that wall was another, and then another, on his way to the western gate. In a move that others would emulate on horses and motorcycles, they say he mounted a water buffalo, and headed west.[4] The gatekeeper at the outer wall would not open for him, but scolded, "You cannot leave us, and take all your wisdom with you. Before you go, you must write something down. Leave us something!"

Mr. Li dismounted, unpacked his brushes, and began to write,

The way that can be understood is not the enduring way.

The name that can be named is not the enduring and unchanging name.

So begins the timeless *Tao Te Ching*. In plainer speech, we can know *about* the Tao, and have a name *for* it, but who can *know* it? We can only know what the Tao reveals. We can only learn from wonder, so let's dare to wonder – let's explore this Unknown together!

One most wonderful thing about this little book is that no matter how we honestly approach it, it rings true. An atheist reads it and sees common-sense observations on life. A Buddhist might see a book of meditations on unseen mysteries, or a politician, a handbook for staying in power. An Orthodox Christian might see there words about the nature of the Christ in the universe. The *Tao Te Ching* encompasses all of these in its many levels.

The fiftieth verse tells us that,

Between birth and death,
Three in ten follow life
Three in ten follow death,
And people passing through are
also three in ten.
Do you ask why?
They do not know how to live.
Those who do know travel freely,
With no fear of wild beasts.

They are not wounded in battle

The rhinoceros' horn finds no place to thrust,

Nor can the great cats reach them with their claws,

Neither weapons find place to pierce.

How can this be?

Death has no place with them.[5]

In some very ancient monasteries when one of their number dies they leave the body exposed in the tomb until there is nothing left to decay. They then clean the bones, gathering them with others in one room – except the skull which they engrave with the person's the name and dates, etc. – and set it with others who have gone before. When someone first seeks to join that community the first stop is to spend a few weeks in that tomb surrounded by those dozens, or hundreds, of skulls. Having confronted his own mortality, he is prepared to live.

In Lao Tse's verse some follow life, some follow death, and some follow nothing in particular. This is their will, their intention, and not their fate, type, or destiny,

We might say those in the first three are intent on living and taking good care of themselves. Those following life have the same weaknesses as anybody else, but have the craft and cunning to succeed in a Fortune 500 boardroom or a tropical jungle. The world, they will tell you, is their oyster. They should remember that bad oysters can be deadly.

Others clearly follow death. Born under a black moon, they might feel compelled to wear full-color "Born to Lose" tattoos on their arms and some acquire some prison ink as well. If something is dangerous, harmful, or addictive, be sure they've tried it at least twice. Others might not stand out at all, but be sure that, on the day her ship comes in, she's at the train station, and if he finally asks his dream girl out, she's found her dream fiancé.

Of those ten there are also the three "just passing through." Not so greedy of life as fearful of death, they just want to stay out of the way and avoid pain. Death has a terrible hold on all who fear it, and none at all on those who embrace it. These three – like the other six, to be sure – would profit from those monks' time, "visiting the dead." The one greatest cause of failure is the fear of it. Fear of insignificance keeps people from risking significance. Fear of poverty keeps people poor, and fear of dying drives many to an early grave. In fact, the Apostle Paul wrote in his first-century CE letter to the Roman Christians, that it is the dread of death that keeps us in despair. Afraid to die, we never live; afraid to fail, we never see success. Afraid of rejection, we shrink from offering ourselves. So, our lives end as weakly as they began. As Mr. Eliot wrote,

This is the way the world ends.

This is the way the world ends.

Not with a bang, but a whimper."[6]

But there is that *one* – one out of the Sage's ten, who stands out, steps away from these three deathly destinies: free from the greed of the first three, from the excesses of the second, and the cowardice of the third. How? When we embrace the Tao we know life and death. Too much lingo? Consider that some of the most powerful – truly, *the* most powerful – people on this planet are those for whom money and creature comforts are but a passing distraction. As Bob Dylan wrote, "When you got nothing you got nothing to lose." This much would apply either to a monk, whose prayers span the Globe and whose writings influence millions, or a soldier who has left his life behind, and lives only to serve his commander.

A certain hermit in the northern forests of Russia taught, "acquire the spirit of peace, and thousands around you will be saved." Though he lived alone in the forest, enough people flocked out to visit him, and wound up staying, to establish several large communities. Even bears would show up, pay their respects, and go their ways. To this day, wild bears come and go at these monasteries, and even find a place at the table. At another such monastery in more recent years Soviet officials, even Premier Brezhnev, would visit, and see such things as the body of a monk long dead, not only lying intact, but giving off an other-worldly perfume. The officials, shaken, returned to Moscow muttering, "That did not happen – it is not rational! I did not just see that!"[7]

One might say that the bear didn't attack because the monk was free from the "illusion" of this world, or even that there was no bear. The *illusion* is being tied *to* this world, not that it exists. Not that the material realm is not real, but that it is not all there is. It does not *own us*. The bears really were there, and their descendants are there today; and they still visit the monks living there after his tradition.[8] Detachment, alone, is not enough. For death to find no place in us is to be so full of life to leave it no space. (After all, if darkness is no light, and cold, no heat, then what is death but just no life?) When this happens, when we are so truly full of life we get to a place where, as one novice monk recently told a mutual friend, "Miracles? Yeah, they're pretty normal around here!" How do we get there from here?

~§~

A monkey can be a hard little creature to corner. Quick and nimble, he is up the tree before we so much as see him see us. But people who catch monkeys don't chase them. All it takes, in fact, is a scrap of rope, a coconut, and a bit of rice. The coconut is cleaned out, with just a small hole in one end, and a smaller one in the other to make way for the rope. The trappers anchor the shell, drop in some rice, and leave. The clever little monkey sees it, and takes a closer look. Rice is inside, how glorious! His little monkey hand reaches in, wraps a tight fist around some, and discovers he can't get it back out of the hole. The monkey won't let go of his prize, and the hunters won't let go of theirs. At best, he will be spending his life behind bars in a foreign zoo, at worst his living brains will be the centerpiece of a local feast. Of all the uses the little creature could find for an open hand – climb away, pick some fruit, caress his young, scratch an ear, once his hand was grasping the rice, it was good for nothing else but to tie him down. The rice, or his desire for it, had him. The treasure had become the traitor.

~§~

Lao Tse wrote in verse 11 of,

> Thirty spokes fit to the hub;
>
> It is useful because of the socket.
>
> A lump of clay makes the jar;
>
> For the space within, it is useful.
>
> So while profit comes from what is within;
>
> Usefulness comes of the space that allows it.

Is a bowl useful except when it is empty and clean? A field, except when it is cleared and plowed? Or a womb, but when it is ready to receive new life? They are *profitable* when full, but always *useful* when empty. That is, empty, they are filled with endless possibility. We chase after "profit," and our own desires betray us, like the monkey's appetite, and how are we any longer useful, even to ourselves? A friend of mine was an engineer at a nuclear power plant. Just out of school, he was making amazing money. He had bought a new house, sports car, sailboat, and matching his and hers Harley-Davidson motorcycles. He ran out of space to store them all. Then the plant was shut down, and he found himself holding thousands of dollars in goodies he couldn't use, sell, or pay for, and a specialised career he could not pursue. Profitable, for a time, but how useful?

Each spoke, fixed in a wheel, is *profitable*. It has its place, and it fills its function, firmly fixed between hub and rim. The hub is *useful* where it is empty, with its sockets open for spokes and axle. It is committed only to possibility. When the wheel is built and turning it turns on that open center of perfect Nothing – the right shape, size, and inner surface – to allow that Something to be useful. When the Nothing is perfected, it becomes useful for Something in particular. So for us to be useful, we first need to clear ourselves of what doesn't belong, to allow for what does. Like in the monkey's story, we learn to hold everything in an open hand, and not a grasping fist. In truth, that Nothing is our potential; our Emptiness is our worth.

With a new wheel, or an empty jar, we keep the opening covered to keep anything outside from getting in. A little grit or moisture, and the wheel is worse than useless, and the tiniest microbe in the jar can turn the finest foods into poison. So, in ourselves, the monkey releasing his grip to escape is one thing, and watching that his desire not cause him to grasp the rice and be trapped again is another. It is one thing that the wheel or the jar be clean and free, but they must be guarded against what doesn't go there.

Is this only physical? The wheel for the axle, the axle or the wheel; the jar for the grain, the grain for the jar. As a universal principle, the jar is made for the grain, and the grain would be lost without it. The wheel and the axle, likewise: the Yin and the Yang. Spiritually, then, it is just as true. The smallest foreign object, any impurity, can destroy the axle as the hub turns on it, or make the whole jar of grain go bad. The same is true for our minds and spirits. A woman I once knew had been brought up like a fragile doll. Ever the precious one, always the weak child, though she had recovered from her birth accident years before. She would later lose one of her own children quite suddenly, and her sorrow consumed her so completely that she could no longer function and destroyed her every living relationship. It seemed that the simple, wrong, expectation that life was supposed to be nice destroyed her.

Jesus Christ spoke of the grain in the jar when he said, "A little leaven leavens the whole lump," and also that those with clean hearts will see God. The vessel of our being must be clean, and kept spotless. If we called it a matter of life and death, would it be overstated?

~§~

Years ago, meditation brought me a measure of detachment, but I had no real control of my desires, or passions. What felt good, I did. I changed my diet and lifestyle to tune my inner self while smoking dope to reach a "higher consciousness." Self-knowledge, self-control, mindfulness? If anything, mind*less*ness was more the plan. It is not too big a leap to say that without mindfulness the next option is a madness. Some of us get there sooner than others, with many not realising we have lived there for years.

I began acquiring small *siddhis*, or spiritual powers, or the powers began acquiring me. As I sought to disappear into the *All*, I let these siddhis become my guides, minding neither where they came from, nor where they led. I would soon get a clue.

~§~

The mists gathered closer as the moon and stars retreated into the darkening skies. Seeking a spirit guide, I was walking through a cypress bog, at the mercy of the damp, and the *magic*. Would the guide come as a glistening black hawk, a great white crow, or a telepathic raccoon? What hidden wisdom, what powers, would I receive?[9] After eating some psychedelic mushrooms I had followed my impulses to a wooded bog not far from town, parked, and started walking. As the drug's influence grew, so did the impulse that had drawn me there until it seemed to be the guide itself – a mood, or spirit, beginning to permeate my mind.

Urged along, I got back in my car for the drive home. There happened to be a long kitchen knife I had tucked under my seat, leaving my restaurant job. I recognised a hitchhiker out on the road. I pulled over, and he got in. Once underway, that same impulse, like a skulking wolf within, began driving me to pull out the knife and kill him. Why would I even think of such a thing? I kept both hands on the wheel as I resisted, struggling to block the images from my mind until we got back to town and he went his way. I saw him a few days later, and he said he had felt a sinister presence in that car that had near scared the life out of him. What had happened? I'll leave that to others to explain, except to say that truth can out-weird fiction. Maybe that's why people find Stephen King's stuff soothing. It is still frightening to think of how close that night, and my life, came to a really macabre end.

"Such a nice young man" I was. Did I know myself? Was I all that nice, or more a predator? Always on the lookout for the next thrill, yet telling myself I was a more noble, "religious" kind of beatnik. After all, I was not as one of these third-wave, "plastic flower children," such shallow thrill-seekers! I read Oriental philosophies, meditated, and was a *vegan. So* proud I was of my quest to lose my ego! All this, with prison and death around any corner. Like the monkey with the coconut, I just hadn't worked out that open hand.

Through my teen years what I learned was more for certainty than wonder. Having the right answers was the thing; the right questions, not so much. Only a passing nod to the Reality behind it all. One sure lesson in that world of certainty is that mere ideas can't sustain life, especially when stacked like mere trophies. Life in that world was drier, bleaker, and more meager, than my spirit could bear.

A concert had been my escape. Neil Young was on stage at a 30,000 seat auditorium. A fat, yellow cigarette was passed my way. Curious, I took a pull of its smoke – and a few more as the music progressed. The smoke and the sound formed chords of their own, which flowed right through my being. When the amplifiers finally fell quiet I felt I was telepathic with the universe.

For many, a bit of history: The time between the early Sixties into the Seventies was a time for experimenting. First were the Beatniks – the word coming from *beatific,* or blessed. These were philosophers, poets, musicians, and deep thinkers, generally: Life is meaningless, so let's do something with it. Drugs – marijuana, cocaine, amphetamines, and heroin – played a part. Next came the

Hippies, or, *Flower Children*. Romantic optimism, free love, freestyle existence. Drugs were more central as a means to unite with the Spiritual. LSD, *acid,* had been synthesised, and it soon became the Next Big Thing. Thousands went to California – especially one neighborhood in old San Francisco – to begin building a new world of peace and love for all. Their new world crashed violently. Being spiritual really worked out as getting high, and between adulterated – or too-powerful – acid, and other drugs used to replace it when scarce, a lot of people took on some permanent damage. Some died from the drugs, some are in mental hospitals to this day, and some were raped or murdered. Volunteer free clinics were set up to handle the steady stream of casualties as hospital emergency rooms filled with overdose cases. "Free love" comes with a price.

The hope had been that the more "good vibes" we could generate the better we could realign the Earth. At best, we just managed to make it *look* realigned for a few hours. "Trippers" looked to connect with deity, with the universe itself, one another, or the family pet for that matter. Connected. Some claimed to have found God and followed that voice to do violent, horrible things. Others became disciples of smooth-tongued messiahs who would lead them into slavery, pedophilia, suicide, and murder.

In the middle of this, I had started reading from people who had been experimented with these things before me. Some were university profs first discovering LSD. Some were young politicos, one a priest who, one of his students said, had decided there was a lot more fun on the wild side giving out his take on Zen than pastoring a flock who likely believed more of their Christian faith than he did. And there was Lao Tse.

A Creative Writing class out in California was taking on a life of its own. The professor was popular enough that the university had rented a movie theater to seat all the students, and he started talking about his own blend of traditional Hindu, Chinese, and Japanese religion, mind science, and psychedelics. As with any class, those who, ah, prepared beforehand likely acquired the teaching more readily. The lectures wound up in a bright purple book in my local bookstore.

His students found that class so inspiring that they camper-ised a bunch of vehicles – complete, of course, with the bright and happy colors of the day – and hit the road with him as a kind of a beatnik salvation show. More people joined up and the caravan grew as they criss-crossed the US with their teacher's laid-back blend of Yoga, Zen, and current events. After a year or so of Gypsy life they had enough interested people to start a communal farm. The land they bought was in the next county over from where I was living, in an Army-sponsored military school.

So one afternoon a young cadet in his starched, creased, and polished Uniform of the Day stepped out of his Proper Protestant Sunday service to see a psychedelic caravan of laughing, waving, gypsy beatniks heading along the main street in a gleaming parade of yellows, greens, and purples, with mystical mandalas. This was too good to be true!

I ran out into the street to hitch a ride with them. My creased and polished clean-cut-ness must have been as much a shock to these West-Coast kids as their own shaggy-bedangled selves were to the proper folks in this Deep-South farm town. Finally, one couple pulled over in – would you believe - an old US Army van they had rigged with bed, stove, and bookshelves, and let me ride with them out to their new home, *in* their home. Meeting the closest followers of my favorite philosopher, and hearing some of their stories, I was in another world. To this star-struck teenager these people were In It To Stay. They had tuned in, turned on, and dropped out of the Dream – freed their hands from the coconut – and were building a new life out in the open, bound together with a common hope for a new world.

With all the conflict in those days between the long-haired Hippie People and what they thought all the crew-cut Military folks were about, and the Military folks and their idea of what the Hippies were thinking, etc., there was far too much time spent that afternoon, with this person or that, explaining what I was doing, what I was wearing, and why my hair was so short if I wasn't in the Army. Yes, and was I a cop, asked at least twice, and surely wondered by all. The sun started to dip and one of the people gave me a ride out to the county road, and I was able to hitchhike back to campus in time to stay out of trouble. It had been a day.

A couple of years later they were growing corn, sorghum, soy, and other foods. They had tractors, road vehicles, and their own mechanics' shop, packing plant, medical clinic, doctor, lawyer, and midwife. The marrieds had cabins while the singles still shared big barracks tents. A businessman would have seen this as a throwback to the plantation days but everyone there was living an adventure.

To me, this seemed ideal. Not getting paid could be a problem, but not needing it would rather even things out. Being part of an ongoing group of like-minded folks sounded good also, and I had been reading this teacher's books for a few years by then. He blended ideas together in a friendly, authoritative way that was easy to accept, and made perfect sense to those of us who heard him.

By this time, the whole aim in my beatnik life was to be fully aware, and free of thought, conflict, or concern: permanently high, with my mind absorbed into the vastness of the Universe. I was living alone like a master-less apprentice Zen monk, if there is such a thing: reading, meditating, working pick-and-shovel labor jobs, and living on rice and water. After having spent time on their farm a couple of times, I was preparing to move up there to live after the first of the year, and give my "thing," my obedience, my identity, over to the teacher.

It was December.

~§~

There is an old story about a child, freezing on a dark city street, with only some matches to sell. The crowds had left, and one by one the child would begin to strike a match, stare into its glow, and imagine being in a warm room full of light and cheer, before the cold overtook her, and she died. Like with that child, our own matches all too soon burn away, don't they?

~§~

A nagging conscience: For all my chanting, dancing, sitting, fasting, and doping to get free of the material plane, I had copped out. Rather than spend Saturday with my parents (and deal with their concerns), I had taken a day job at a strip mall, playing Santa Claus. First I was patting myself on the back for my integrity, and then I was endorsing the whole, commercial Santa Claus myth for just a few dollars, and using this to dodge my parents! Oh, well, just one more guilt to store away for later.

So, decked out in garish polyester – red suit, white beard and all that, I was waddling my two-pillow belly up and down the sidewalk, handing out candy with my best, "Ho-ho-ho." Odd, how Santa laughs so much and says so little! All the shoppers were glad to exchange a cheerful, "Merry Christmas," with me, as if I were their old, dear friend. The store sponsoring the gig, though, had no lockers, so my keys and such wound up in a purple Chivas Regal bag dangling off my belt loop. When the façade was over reality slapped me twice. At a time when the words, "dirty," and "hippie," seemed inseparable, folks weren't nearly so glad to see a skinny young man with his own beard as they were a padded actor with a borrowed one. For a slightly bigger problem, when I had reached for my personal items, the bag was gone. Now, here it was mid-December, this city's-edge shopping center was some serious mileage south of my mid-town cottage, and winters there are the damp, clammy-to-the-bone chilly variety. This was a problem.

I was able to catch a ride to an old enclosed shopping mall so I could look for familiar faces inside instead of watching the winter sun disappear from the side of the frozen highway. Searching amongst the busy shoppers, though, there was not a friend in sight. Then, out of nowhere, there was a full-on gorgeous hippie chick standing square in front of me, complete with dark wavy hair, soft brown eyes, and sequined red gypsy dress, asking, "Hey, are those army boots you're carrying?"

This was the most befuddling thing she could have said, whoever this lady was – boots, what? Was this an opener, or was she about to go off on me for having something to do with the military? Was her boyfriend about to show up with some friends, looking for a beatnik to pound? "Uh, yeahhh," was the best I could do. "I thought so – my husband is in the Army. I want you to meet him!"

"Wait a minute," I was thinking, "First this dazzling chick walks up to me out in the mall with a pick-up line, and now she wants me to meet her husband?" This evening was getting stranger by the moment, but she looked cool enough, and I still did need a ride.

The Hippie Chick, I learned, was Lynda, and her soldier husband, Bob[10]. A couple of years before, he had been drafted for military duty – "invited" to endure three years of bush-war insanity, or die trying, in South Asia, and that for no defined reason. They'd read the letter, hit the road, and kept moving. They dodged local, county, state, and federal police agencies around the country until, somewhere out West, they had met some "Jesus Freaks."

A Jesus Freak, back in the 70's, was a young hippie, beatnik, or other self-styled misfit, who had become a Christian, often through some really bizarre circumstances, and stayed in the "scene," to the point of keeping the same appearance and lifestyle – only without the drugs and promiscuity – rather than copy the "established" norms. Some, like the folks Bob and Lynda had met, were living in communes of various kinds. From getting to know some of them, my new friends had been converted, and had lived on their farm for a while. Then Bob realised they couldn't keep evading the police, and it wasn't really honest, anyway. He went to the local Draft Board[11] to turn himself in, and after all their fear, drama, and fugitive miles somebody had lost his records. Nobody had even been looking for them after all. Because of his honesty they arranged for him to serve his enlistment in the US and be free and clear.

All this came out as we were talking at the mall, and on the way back to my house, where we talked well into the night about police and politics, about gardening, children, travel, and all kinds of common interests. I started to notice somebody else was there. I could see where Bob, Lyn, and young Kim – some friends' young kid they were watching – were, of course, but there was another person in there with us.

Suddenly, and here is where we leave the Mundane, this somebody was there – not to be seen, but to be known. Just over to the left, beyond the woodstove, was a *person* – a *presence*. It's still hard to describe all these years later, but who hasn't been alone in a room, and known that somebody was there? Now turn that up a few notches. This was no "seems to be," and somehow I knew this person's identity: He was *Truth.* Now, I was really invested in creating my own truth, as most of us are, and the idea of a revealed and delivered package, was *not* what I was looking for, and less, if this *Truth* is a person! Concepts are negotiable. Principles we can discuss. A *person* is just there. With all the "truths" I had been scraping together, I had been making my way through the dark with a book of paper matches, and suddenly comes the sunrise. The problem was, I had gotten kind of comfortable with those matches! They made pretty colors, and I decided which one to strike, and when. When the sun comes up, it's up.

Lynda reminded Bob of the time, and Bob said, "before we go, how about let's pray together?" As spiritual as I saw myself to be, I agreed. We all bowed our heads. Bob said something. Then Lyn did. I saw the trap: this was a "conversational prayer," which some

Christians use. Everybody had a say, or else everybody just politely sits and waits! I said, "Lord, your will be done."

They left, and I got some sleep. The next morning, I woke up praying. A great conversion? Nothing of the sort! It was all, "Lord, I know I said what I said last night, but, well, ya see, there's *this lady*, ya see, and, well, I know the way you do relationships isn't the same way I like to do things, so, ah, how about, maybe, a kind of, uhh, a rain check for a little while?" I went out to see this lady at her work. She was doing some embroidery on my jean jacket, which was a thing then. As soon as I walked in, she went back to the office, got my jacket, and handed it to me. "I've just kinda lost any interest in any kind of romantic thing with anybody for a while," she said, "and I don't know why," Considering my thoughts on waking up that morning, I had a feeling I knew, and I really didn't want to!

In those great old Roadrunner cartoons, the Coyote was finding himself in positions like standing where a high ledge had just been. He wouldn't fall until he noticed there was nothing under his feet. I felt like the ground under me had just disappeared. The ground under my own feet – what I believed, my reasons for doing what I did, for being who I was – was gone. In truth, it had never been there at all.

So, there, in my living room, was, "Truth," and in a particular location. Not something I preferred, but there it was, not to be ignored. So either what I was about was *true*, or not, and if not. If not, then it was all a lie, and built on lies. Either way, I was a dead man. To follow Truth meant leaving behind the partial truths I had collected. Life as I knew it was over. Otherwise, I would know my life was a pretense - no real life, at all, no excuse for breathing.

The next night, I was talking with a young Jesus freak, and told him I agreed with something he had said, though not, "coming from a Christian place" – that what he had said seemed to be a lot more Common Sense than being only "Christian." A quiet thought, though – like a voice – suddenly spoke to the very depths of me, asking, "Why?" Not a question I could answer. I knew what I had been up to, the mess I'd made, the pain, the damage done to others, and myself, from all my mindlessness. I had nothing to offer, nothing to recommend. There was no rain check. "Lord, I give up. Snuff me if you want to. I'm yours!" It would be no surprise to see that old, worn, carpet rushing up to meet my falling face.

It was still December.

The Commune

There is a place in the Christian Bible that says, "it is a fearful thing to fall into the hands of the living God." I had been part of a culture that, for all its rosy optimism, did, in fact, cause a lot of damage. We can speak of free love, but soon discover that "love" was not self-giving but self-pleasing, with all the broken hearts, broken lives, abortions and suicides that follow. It is just not possible for millions of naive young people to pick and choose what kinds of narcotics and psychedelics to load into their heads, and everybody walk away from the experience healthy, happy, and whole, or even breathing.

I did taste death that night as it seemed a new mind was looking out from these same two eyes. I was clear of drug effects I hadn't even realised were there, thinking clearly and objectively as somehow a new man, and yet all the more myself.

The next three weeks brought a whirlwind of changes. I visited my parents. "Why do you still have that *beurd?*" My grandmother was speechless, overjoyed to have me back. Ways opened up to pay out my rent, and Bob and Lynda introduced me to some friends of theirs in an urban commune nearby. Then, right when I had planned to be moving to the farm, three weeks to the hour from "snuff me," I was dropping my bags on that communal living-room floor. I was home.

New Year's Eve, midnight.

~§~

Now, it was plain to see that my life of seeking sensual bliss had ended. Real bliss, real ecstasy, is about living into Truth, and Truth living into oneself. All I had known were opinions, based on other opinions. Most of when we "know" anything it means we like our opinion of somebody else's opinion. The more strongly we hold to it, the tighter the monkey grips the rice, and the more we suffer. We might decide God is thus-and-so. We're wrong. God, limited isn't. If a thoughtful person asks if God exists, the answer must be, "no." Who can comprehend Someone so vast, or define an "existence" open enough to describe such a state of Being? I was finding that *Truth* is a whole new way of life.

~§~

Learning by Forgetting

A few days after I had gotten into a discussion with one of the other guys there I was in the house pickup trick with the house pastor. He told me, "I hear you and Tommy got into a discussion the other night. Now, I'm not going to debate you on it, but I want to let you know that we don't receive *that teaching* (my opinion) here, so I'm going to ask you not to be talking it around, because it will just confuse people." Of course, I just said, "okay." Inside, though, I was flipping out. "God! Why did you give me a pastor who does not believe this *most basic truth?*" I did not understand "first principles." [12]

When we pray, closed questions don't get answered too often. A friend of mine was in his third year of undergrad studies at a school which was really big on that, "truth," so I went to see him. We decided to hold a series of debates to work out the right answer. We met three times. He took the "preferred" position, and I, the other. Out of three debates, I won three. *I did not want to.*

Walking back to the house, once again it seemed my feet were doing that same old, where-did-the-ground-go, soft shoe. First, my acquired beliefs, and now the ones I had grown up with. Remember the hermit crab? I prayed, "God, what is going on?" Open questions get answers.

In a sense of calm gentle, instruction, the words came, "Just keep reading your Bible the way you have been, and be prepared to change when I say 'switch.'" I could deal with that.

Now, in the Zen tradition there is a story of two monks travelling through the city after a heavy rain. Along the way they saw an attractive young woman in long, flowing silks as she hesitated to walk across the muddy street. The elder monk summarily gathered her up and across the flood, and then back onto her feet on the footpath. The monks then walked on quietly for three more blocks. The novice spoke up: "Elder, please explain to me this mystery. We are taught it is not good even to look on a woman, and you carried this one in your arms!" The old monk paused, smiled, and replied, "I set her down back there. Are you still carrying her?" In his dispassion, he had not touched her though he carried her; the novice had not touched her, yet had never let go.

For the monkey, the rice is not the problem. Rice is good. The coconut shell is just where the rice is. His greed in grasping it so tightly is his undoing. In an open hand, he would have the rice, and would be free to do as he would with hand and rice. *Usefulness*. So, I would read a little bit every night, and every night grasp onto parts that beautifully confirmed what I believed amongst much longer passages I could not understand. At each of these I would simply pray to understand later, and keep on reading. After two or three weeks, one night, there came, "Now, switch!" I started reading from the other "as if," and the whole picture began fitting together perfectly[13]. I had been reading, before, knowing what it was I expected to see, and what little I saw was colored with paints from that point of view. Being open to the text saying what it said, my understanding became useful, like the monkey's open hand.

It is a perpetual double negative. We can gain only by giving up, and only give up without grasping. We plant seeds, bury them, forget them. They prosper. We keep digging and watching them, they rot. Seeds, wisdom, life.

We don't just let go of opinions. Life is more than opinions. We worked in crews at the same jobs, with the pay going to a common purse. Besides paying bills, we could help others who needed a bed, a coat, or a meal. Altogether, at the different houses, several thousand people came off the streets, got clean, and learned to take account of their lives. Our hands, being empty, were useful.

One night a man and woman came to visit. He had returned from the military madness in Vietnam, and brought some of it back with him. He worked as a meat cutter. They had fallen behind on their rent and the landlord had locked them out until they paid up.

In a few days he got his paycheck, and they got their home back. Then she decided to leave when he said he wouldn't marry her. The following Saturday she came back to stay with us until she made arrangements. I got picked to escort her back to fetch her bags. Easy enough, except for the boyfriend didn't seem to be in on the plan. Just at the apartment, as I was asking her, "are you sure you got everything," he showed up. There was his girlfriend, in his living room with some hippie, and all her suitcases by the door. He came unglued, just, boom. He was going to kill me, kill her, and slice us up, maybe not in that order. He was big enough, mad enough, and likely crazy enough to go through with it. A kind of holy peace assured me that no harm would come. His threats died down from bluster to grumble, and he left. We gathered up the bags and walked back to the house. This was *Te*.

The commune effort folded after a few years. Life, since, involved me with folks of nearly every belief and tradition out there, with each playing a part in my life with its own beauty, truth, and humanity. "Now, switch," turned out to be more about not attaching – about being open to not already knowing – than just reading correctly. To learn, we embrace our ignorance, to be filled, we must be empty; to be profitable, we must first be useful. To be free of the trap, the monkey must set aside his lust for gain. Unattached, we become free from the illusion that what we see is all there is. So, the desire – the passion, to grasp onto it loses its grip on us.

From Detachment to Mastery

I found myself working with folks in the streets, jails and prisons, arranging Christmas gifts for their kids, and helping out where I could. No phony costume this time. Real presents. Real life.

When people are in need, there is always one thing they need the most. Whatever the need, whatever the crisis, the one great need is *nothing*. To be any help to anybody, to be a friend, we need first to let go. All attachments, all desires, passions, or agendas – gone. Carrying an agenda into a prison cell or a sick room is worse than carrying a deadly weapon; there is no telling the harm it can do. Anybody can bring an agenda, but a friend comes with empty hands – asking nothing, expecting nothing, just being there.

It is only from bringing that nothing, like the empty space in the wheel, that connection can happen. We quiet ourselves, listen to others, and give them the space to be who they are. Dogs are interesting. They can be the most loyal friends around. A charming prayer goes, "Lord make me the person my dog thinks me to be," and people can train them to do all kinds of things. Training a cat, however, is another thing. The cat might watch us *try* to train it, but only until it goes to find something else more interesting, like a paw that needs to be licked. The dog, and the cat's owner – no agenda, no demands.

Living is learning, and learning is a conversation – a relationship. There are some things we know, some things we don't, and more that we don't even realise are there to be known – including what we think we know. Louis XV of France had as a motto, "I am but a child; I need to be taught," and Mr. Suzuki[14] wrote, as I understand him, that the one crucial step to learning anything is knowing nothing.

So, being of service being in the conversation – requires *nothing*, and learning also requires *nothing* in three particular forms. We need to be detached, first of all; free to discover what there is to know. Does the teacher or the text say what we want to hear? It doesn't matter. We can discuss, question, or compare how what we believe lines up with what we are learning, dispassionately. What we know may or may not be correct, but it is never complete. In the ways it is not complete, whatever is left out can make the rest deceptive.

We empty the pot and scrub it, in order to fill it; we bore the wheel hub, and mill it for the axle. Nothing in the way, nothing rough, nothing nasty. We clear out what doesn't belong, and make way for what does. Nothing in the way, and nothing hidden. We loose our grip on what we know to make space for what we don't. A burr or grit in the hub, and its life is short. A pot with the smallest crack or speck of filth in the vessel, and its contents can be wasted, or poisoned.

So, we need to be *mindful.* If detachment is the opening in the wheel, and dispassion is polishing it smooth, then mindfulness is the lid on the pot, and the seal on the hub. detachment is perfected in dispassion, and mindfulness is fulfilled in mastery.

In the inner world, we practice a kind of mindfulness to guard our detachment and maintain dispassion, so we can achieve real mastery of ourselves and our practice. Evagrios followed his Greek teachers in saying that before we know anything we must first know ourselves.

~§~

Something about Onions:

So, we ask, what am I, as a person? My clothing – is that me? My likes, dislikes, beliefs, opinions? True, that tomato can isn't the crab, but where is the actual person in all this? Peel an onion. Where's the core? Take off a layer, then another. Find the core – where is the onion? Where is real self? Or is it the "self," the *intellect*, peeling the onion?

We want to learn, but what do we learn with? Our minds? What puts the knowledge into our minds? The intellect must be free from inward resistance, coarseness and debris, like the opening in the wheel's hub, and the emptiness of the vessel, but it must be clear to do so. "Know Yourself:" Be familiar with yourself, clear of attachments to opinions, desires, fears, passions, and "mind weeds." No longer attached, we no longer cling to this world's allures and illusions; dispassionate, we do not reach for them. Mindful, we listen, and learn.

The Spirit Book

People in tribes and villages all over the world, wherever they are "isolated" enough to remember who they are as a people, have their own stories about a time in the far past when their ancestors knew Shang-Ti, the One, Sky Father, Great Spirit, or whatever they called their single, all-wise and powerful Deity. The Greeks spoke of "the One" as being above and beyond Zeus, Hera, and the rest, while the Brahmins saw their gods as avatars – living representations – of the Deity beyond the gods.

The legends would typically say that the ancient ones had lost a book this Deity had given them, or that, at any rate, they had failed to keep His teachings, and begun to serving weaker gods out of shame. Yet, through hundreds of generations, the memory still remained of a time when they, as a people, actually knew their Source. In some cases there had been modern-day tribal seers predicting that men of a certain description would one day arrive at a certain place, bringing that book back to them.[15] In one such case, in Burmese mountains where anybody only ever saw each other, this did happen. The tribal elders received them with joy, and the book they brought matched the teachings they had been told were in their own lost book. We have this same book today.

~§~

We all have ancestors – Goth, Chin, Celt, Semite, Bantu, Arawakan, or any combination of hundreds more – with memories and traditions of some kind. When we forget those traditions, we lose an important part of ourselves. Could this be why Lost Innocence, or "simpler times," is so big in the arts, and why the very idea of *connection* resonates with us so deeply? There is that *something*, behind our thinking, missing, half-remembered, never quite brought to mind – a sense of *being* in that place we have always longed for and never seen, wonderful beyond what the imagination could ever hold. We see magnificent cloudscapes, mountain vistas, rolling hills, or the vast expanses of plains, seas, or night skies – each giving us a sense of *home!* We find those deep memories in stories – Middle Earth, or Narnia, or *The Velveteen Rabbit.* Stories of King Arthur, Merlin, Arthur Dent, or Granny Weatherwax give us dreams not for slumber, but to bring us more fully awake.

Between 2,000 and 3,500 years ago, such people as a couple of tent-dwellers in one place, a sheep-herder in another, or a king, a soldier, or a psychic had encounters with a Spirit, talking to them, sometimes causing unpredictable things to happen. These encounters got written down. When put together they turned out to be about the same Spirit. Much was written down, though most was probably not. We find evidence of this in many books – the vedas and gitas, the Tao Te Ching, the Bible, and others, as well as the oral traditions of many bush tribes. Taken together, they have more in common than we can afford to dismiss, and much that speaks to us in our own day.

Some of them come to us as myths of super-men doing battle with deities. More give us aphorisms and precepts. One is unique in that it speaks in verifiable history. At such a time this or that happened, and the names of the witnesses were these. Such data as ancient scrolls and archaeological digs bear the stories out to be historically accurate. This one, or collection of many, is the most controversial of the lot. To most it is simply called the Bible.

It's good history. But it's about people, not just artifacts. Their clothing, diet, or technology might have been different, but they had the same fears, joys, hopes, and pains to deal with. There was also the matter of this God showing up in their lives. These stories spread over some four thousand years and five million square miles, yet each encounter shows up as some further insight into what this God is about, as if one person, and not forty or more[16], had written it all. Some of the accounts are exciting, even funny, and some disturbing. Some are hard to understand, but who steps 3,000 years into the past without a touch of jet lag? The slower come the conclusions, the more quickly, the understanding.

The more we read, and the less we expect, the more we see, as it resonates as one *word*, encompassing many. I have found, of course, many contradictions, each one getting in the way of my own agendas. We know about agendas, don't we?

A couple floats across the dance floor – practiced, fluid, supple, free to respond to one another's movements, to flow within the music, to use the plain boards beneath them like a swallow dances in the air. His rhythm sends her twirling, as her skirts flare outward as birds of paradise taking flight . He frees her to move with ease, her own freedom enabling him to guide their euphoria across the room.

Even so, we read, we question, we listen. We dance. We engage the text like a dance partner, in the give and take of a waltz, a tango, a ballet. We learn as we give up on knowing, gain by releasing what is in our grasp. We increase in knowledge only by not figuring it out; we learn what is right through being wrong. What we *know* is the booby prize. What counts is what we *become.*

A young monk told his abbot one evening, "I am not going back to chapel anymore. I am just not getting anything out of it." When asked to explain, he replied, "every night, we listen to the readings and we chant the Psalms. By the time I get back to my cell, I have forgotten which Psalms we chanted or what was even read. It's just no use."

He simply replied, "do not be hasty, my son. Do me a small favor first. Go pick up one of those two hand baskets from under that tree. Every time you come to prayers, first go down to the river by your hut and fill that basket with water, and when you come, pour it into that rain barrel. Do this first, then we will talk about your complaint." The young man thought that surely this was the most unusual thing he had heard this man say, , but his abbot was not a foolish man, so he followed his counsel. Several months passed, then a year, and still he kept up this exercise. Finally he was asked what he had learned.

"Learned?" he replied. "The weave of this basket is obviously far too open to hold a bit of water, so no matter how I hurry the barrel still gets nothing. What am I supposed to learn from this?"

"Look in your basket, my son," said the elder. "What is in it?" Surely he had taken leave of his senses! Hadn't he just said the basket was empty?

"See for yourself, Father – see, it is completely empty!"

"Now," the elder told him, "go look at the other basket, still under the tree. What is in it?"

He looked under the tree, and saw a basket that was nasty, buggy, and half rotted away, with spider webs, dead leaves, dried centipedes, and maggot bugs, and so he said, "Father, it is full of everything filthy!"

"My son, so it is within us. No matter what we retain, the holy words cleanse our hearts and refresh us." What we take in stays with us and becomes our thoughts – whether mind weeds, the quietness that stunts them and renders us useful, or the crops which make us truly profitable.

~§~

The Master and the Priest

An old farmer was always showing up, morning and evening, in the back of the old village chapel. He would linger awhile, each time, and then go on his way. A new priest had come in. Noticing these odd visits for a few weeks, he approached him.

"Hello, sir. You come here often, I see."

"Yes, Father, this is rather a habit, since my dear wife's passing."

"Yet what do you do? I never see you with a prayer book, or even a knotted prayer rope!"

"No, Father, I have never been taught such things."

"So, then, do you come to meditate, or contemplate the Mysteries?"

"No, never learned such things, either."

"Then, and please don't think me rude, but what is it you do here, every morning, and evening?"

"I come here. I look at Him," he said. "He looks at me. We are happy!"[17]

Know Yourself

Any kind of mastery takes mindfulness. We look at a bodybuilder or a ballerina. Their posture and motion are entirely different from most people. These are athletes who have a relationship with every fiber of their bodies, and every motion reflects this. Besides the grace and ease of their motions, they are capable of things we "normal" people can't imagine. The ballerina stretches her body to reflect flawless control, and a bodybuilder might lift half a dozen ballerinas in the air with the same ease. As they exercise they come to know, and develop, their bodies. As the body, so the spirit, two sides of the same coin.

The ancient monk, Evagrios, wrote, "You cannot attain pure prayer… agitated by constant cares; for prayer means the shedding of thoughts.[1819] "Here, again, we see the useful, and profitable, mind. Real prayer is self-mastery, at the beginning, in the end, and all in between. What can we offer, that we don't own? We own what we know.

We only know what we learn, and learning takes attention – especially for getting to know our real selves. Sure, we have a false self, one for every occasion, that can even fool us if we're not careful. Like a politician, it feeds on our desires, regrets, and strongly-held opinions to gain, hold, and increase power over all it sees. First of all, it hijacks the real self. How hard is it for a young woman to be an adult to her parents, or for parents to accept their son as a peer? The parent roles and the child roles have their scripted conversations, while the people, themselves, struggle for a way to break out and have a real conversation – to really know each other.

If we look back at Lao Tze's nine in ten we remember that whether we pass our lives fleeing death, denying death, or bracing for death, it is still the fear of death that dominates us. This false self seems to be simply a mechanism, a reflex, to avoid any kind of "ego death." This might be hurt feelings, lost status, humiliation, or simply a change in habits. Forgiveness is essential.

It doesn't take a lot of effort to dwell in regrets and resentment, and not a lot more to agitate over desires and anxieties, and these are where most of the mind weeds come from that clog our minds until clear thinking is a fleeting fantasy. Whatever the mental health field might call it, let's call it the Blanket Reflex. It has to keep control of the security blanket, and when it feels threatened, pop, goes the blanket, right over our heads. Somebody knows he needs to stop smoking, but smoking is a habit, and habits are comfortable. Up pops the blanket. There is a dangerous relationship. Even a bad relationship feels safer than none at all, and so the Reflex keeps her there come hell or high water. One side to the kind of mindfulness we're dealing with means acknowledging what is so, even what we would otherwise have "sleep-walked" through, wrapped in that soft, constraining blanket.

To really know oneself, first of all, means not clinging to a graven self-image. However we choose to see ourselves decides how we interpret our universe, and that interpretation then re-enforces our self-image. A "good person" will overlook some serious flaws; a "loser" will ignore a lot of strengths. Of course, a lot of variations, and an awful lot of details, show up here. Knowing ourselves requires attention – mindfulness – from an attitude of detachment and dispassion.

A lot of people seem to think that self-knowledge is just living in the obvious – self-concern, self-love, self-consciousness. How do we look, and how can we look better? How do we feel, and how can we feel better? What do we want, and how do we get more? These concerns grow up like weeds until our minds are no longer useful, and blanket our vision so we cannot see what is ahead.

How do we look, or feel? What do we have? These are incidental matters. Are we not who we are, regardless of how our hair is trimmed, or whether we are tired or alert? We can also pick up an opinion, and consider it to be who we are. Were we somebody else before that? If so, who? A marriage, promotion, scar, or amputation – these all relate in their own way. Who are we, though, and how does that person deal with these things? The task at hand is to get past the accidents and the incidents to get to the essence of who we, really, are.

If we drove a car, with an eye just to the incidentals, it would be a mercy that we never found our way to the street. With all our attention on the seat covers, radio, and visor mirror, we would be better off blindfolded. But, being savvy drivers like we are, we keep our minds on where we are going, what's around us, and the engine condition. So, let's look at this whole dispassion thing, about not letting our desires run us. Where does this life lead? To the grave, no? Do dead people party? You have probably heard about the two men who decided to take their treasures with them when they died, but in case you didn't, there was one who demanded that all his money be buried with him. Well enough, then, his widow slipped his bank card into his burial suit pocket. The other dying man gave his friend a bottle of expensive whiskey he had never opened, with the request that he pour it on his grave. Another friend asked him later if he had done it. "Of course I did. You knew I would. Of course, such a fine fellow as Frank wouldn't mind too much that I passed it over my kidneys first."

No, the departed don't seek pleasure, and the less our own attention is set on what our appetites and egos demand, the more we can deal with what we really need, down inside. The first step to wisdom, after all, is to remember that we, too, will die, and embrace it.[20] We all pass through the same door, and whoever dies with the most toys, well, drops off the most toys on the way out. Max effort, zero gain.

But how can we navigate what we can't see? "He that loves his life," like the greedy monkey, "will lose it," just like Lao Tse's "nine of ten." To live, to know ourselves, we must embrace our own deaths. Until then, everything is a duck and a dodge, with that Blanket Reflex protecting our egos from death, and us from living. Do we seek death? No, but we must embrace it.

The good news is that it is all good news. "This current distress" has an ending. Nothing in this life – nothing we can see, touch, taste, hear, or feel – is here to stay, and we're not in it for that, if we're to be of the One in Ten. After all, if we have something we can't trust, is it better to know it, or let it surprise us? So, like the Apostle says, everything will be shaken, "that those things which cannot be shaken may remain." What can be shaken dies, so what can't can be revealed. What can be shaken? Our appetites can be shaken, surely, as we see them appear for no reason, and often disappear for less. Our fears, our opinions, surely, can change, and our affections. Is it wise, then, to let such fickle impulses guide our lives? How many people end their marriages from thinking it was all about feelings, and know nothing of love? One more layer of the onion, and another, but who can find the core? The ultimate mindfulness, then, is becoming aware of the invisible within us.

As a young boy, I was sure that fishing was just a lure on a line. So, with all the folks who had been bringing fish out of those waters for thousands of years before me, and all the books and magazines there were about other people's experience, I could not imagine what there was to learn about something so simple as fishing. So, I would fish, and catch a few, here and there, and none all that big. Then came the competition fishermen with their fast boats, sonars, and studied technique, who had devoted years of study and practice to learning the particular ways of the fish they were after. I really should not have been surprised when they started pulling out fish the size of a big man's leg, the likes of which I never dreamed even swam in any fresh water south of Lake Erie. These fishermen were masters. They knew where to look, and how to listen.

A real, "master" has mastered himself, by being mastered by his discipline. Only then is he qualified to teach others[21], whether it is a simple dance step, or the highest forms of prayer. When Sir Isaac Newton said, "If I have seen farther, it is only by standing on the shoulders of giants," even that line came from another.[22] All scholarship, science, or technology is just so many bricks that we stack into whatever shapes we find profitable. We have so many ideas, so many elements to our existence, and that's it. Eighty-eight notes on a piano, about sixty on a guitar. Bach, Beethoven, or Bieber, any song or symphony is pieced together from just so many notes, chords, and themes. We can be masters of all other things, and yet be slaves without control of our own thoughts and desires. However many parts fashion our outward world, unless we master the world within it is all for nothing.

And mastering this inward thing called prayer is also – of course – a two-way street. *Whatever we master masters us.* A pianist, after years of practice, sits down, sets her hands to the keys. The technique is second nature, the notes take a life of their own, and the music flows. She has become the music, as the talent of her teachers, and theirs, sings out through the hammered harp at her fingertips. A master craftsman's skills and knowledge, from the many generations of the craft before him, guide his hands as he guides the skill, so that he can say that it is the craft doing the work through him. The old farmer in our story knew more about prayer than the young priest, for all his studies, and was mastered by prayer in ways the young priest could not dream.

First of all, he was quiet. None of the, "Hey, God, you really gotta hear this," or, "Let me get this prayer thing out of the way." The best friends often have the best conversations with the fewest words said. Recently, I was in a meeting with a widely-respected abbot. For all the things I had thought to say, questions I wanted to ask, if I ever met him, none of it mattered so much, or was, really, appropriate, when I was at the table with him except to ask his blessing. Truth be known, for all the man's scholarship, knowledge, and wisdom, and all his connections, I really would rather have his prayers!

What, really, is *prayer?* Is it about reading off a list of troubles, and telling God what to do about them? Just to tell the All-Knowing what we think only we know, and throw in some religious jargon every so often? Who shows up in the boss's office with a bunch of "well ya know," "seems to me," and, "ya really oughtta?" Who appears before royalty with a shopping list? In fact, who runs his mouth before even a county judge, but finds out what a great idea it wasn't?

Neither is it some self-involved, train-of-consciousness, psychological exercise. These serve, first of all, to establish mind weeds with ever-deeper roots and the best of fertilisers. Some think of it, also, as some effort to stay fresh and spontaneous, with every thought and phrase original. Considering how many people have lived, or now live, in this world, and how rarely a thought crosses our minds that we even think is original, the odds for an originally personal idea, or prayer, are about even with tripping on a stone and landing on the moon.

Interestingly, when Jesus Christ's followers asked him to teach them how to pray he started off by saying, "When you pray, say..." They already had set prayers they said at certain times, and he respected that. He did not chide them for not being "original." In fact, he gave them a particular prayer to recite that teaches as much as it "supplicates."

Our Father in Heaven, all praise be to Your name.

May Your Kingdom come, Your will be done,

On Earth, as in Heaven.

Give us our bread each day,

And forgive our sins, as we forgive others' against us.

Do not lead us into trials, but deliver us from the evil one.

~

Why so few words? And why these words? Jesus told them, "Your Father in Heaven knows what you need before you ask," and so for us not to expect Him to hear us the more, for speaking the more. (So why did one of his "sent ones" say to, "pray without ceasing," and how would this be possible? All shall be revealed, as they say!)

There was a certain Jewish sect in ancient days who were really heavy on recruiting. They would make public spectacles of their personal prayers so as to say, "See there? This is how to do it!" They would even dress up in their religious best and hire trumpeters just to stand out more. What makes all this more sad, and more of a lesson to us all, is that this movement started a way to encourage others to take their own religious practices more seriously and wound up using their façade for political position to oppress others. Jesus used their example as a warning, teaching his followers to keep their prayers personal, even to the point of hiding in a closed room to pray.

His point? That prayer is, first of all, simple, and then, quiet – outwardly, and especially, within.

~§~

While those with much experience, and much *Te*, can stand for hours in silence, in inexpressible communion with the Unseen, most of us do well to stay five minutes. Some recent experimenters left their subjects in a quiet room, with no distractions or stimulation beyond their own thoughts, and a set of electrodes in place to give them a painful shock if they pressed a button they were given. Nearly half of them soon began pressing it to avoid being left to their own thoughts. This even persisted when the pain level was cranked to higher levels.[23]

~§~

Each of us has any number of thoughts stirring about, and not even our own thoughts. The harder we try to think clearly the more these weeds keep cropping up. "Mind weeds," or choking vines, more like it, come from any number of sources, and the more we feed them the more they spread. C. S. Lewis reworks Homer's *Odyssey* to create a story of sailors leaving home to seek out exiled heroes. Along the way they face some truly mysterious dangers. The worst is a deep fog which causes all who pass through it to see their dreams come true. Not the warm, waking fantasies, the sailors are warned, but those from the best-buried parts of the mind. Sure enough, as they sail on, the screams and pleas coming from those sea-hardened veterans are such to turn the hottest blood to icy seawater.[24]

These are the thoughts that haunt us; they hijack our minds when we need them the most. We might gain focus by minding our breathing, or just acknowledging the thought without engaging it. From my experience, these methods simply put the most demanding things on hold to keep showing up like unpaid fines, and taking the time to say, "I see you" to every passing thought only gets us so far.

Washing in Words

Once as a child I had a kind of tiny shade-shifting lizard in a little screen-wire and wood cage the size of a large shoe carton. It ate from a match box, and drank from a bottle top. I got too busy being a brat of a boy, and left off watering it for several days. It shriveled down into a grim little sight –

dry skin shrunken down into its frail ribs and sunken belly, eye sockets dark and hollow, and no more weight than a speck of straw. One very upset little boy gently picked up and prayed for that sapless cadaver – and for forgiveness in neglecting it – setting it down into a little tray of water. Not much time passed before the lizard had absorbed enough water through its skin that it started to recover. Soon it started lapping water with its newly-restored tongue, stretched its re-limbered limbs, and scampered off to the back of the cage as if nothing had ever happened!

Today, too often we find ourselves in such a cage. Our lives seem so dry, our souls, so brittle, and our vision reduced to hollow sockets where ought to be bright eyes full of wonder. We have gotten so accustomed to being dry that we seldom think how thirsty we are.

Somewhere, somehow, we still remember how things are supposed to be. We might be reminded after a long journey, or a nasty experience, how a shower, a swim, or a tall, cool, drink can be more welcome than words can describe. It makes us feel more like *ourselves,* somehow, doesn't it?

In fact, back in the 7th century CE, a certain sage[25] wrote something, well, rather scandalous – we are created for ecstasy! In his Greek language, "ecstasy," meant, "outside-standing," as, "standing outside of oneself." Being completely ecstatic in God makes us fully human, and fully divinised. So, when our ecstasy centers on our own desires, do we become as the animals? No, he said, but the beast fulfills its purposes by following its instincts. We make the beasts our betters when we refuse to follow our purposes. Also, concerning the animals, another saint[26] wrote, "they serve God on their place better than we on ours." When we have parted the veil of our so-called intellect we come to see them as holy, and never treat them as "lower". As another man said, "My dog is better than I, for he has love, and does not judge."

The ancient apostle Paul wrote something to his followers about, "washing in the water of the word." What can this mean? Obviously nobody is bathing in books, and books aren't wet. Most folks couldn't read, and books cost more in that day than real estate. Their whole experience of Scripture was in the chants they would hear at worship. Being bathed in that melodious flow is a wholly different image from climbing into a book with a bar of soap!

Now, we can say that our minds *are* masses of conversations. What will I eat? Where will I live? When will I die? Why am I here? How can I get any work done with all these questions flying around? On, on, and on. "The best-laid plans ..aft gang agley," as they say, so how are we helping with the non-stop commentary? Our minds fill up with these monologues, imagined dialogues, and more gibbering regrets, resentments, and ongoing obsessions than we like to admit to. If we were up-front conscious of them all we'd all go nuts. As it is, they just block our way to real sanity.

Some of this background matter sorts and interprets our experiences: a lot more of it keeps us distracted in any number of directions. Still, we sort whatever occurs outside of our heads by what is happening on the inside, whether we've got a lot of control over that or not.

We all have weeds – and spider webs, dead leaves, dried centipedes, and maggot bugs, for that matter – cluttering up our mind space. They ever multiply, interfere with our "nothing," and destroy our usefulness. Lao Tse's wheel needs its axle socket empty and clean, or it will never turn properly. This has always been true, though our modern experience has its own details and pressures. As one man starting along the journey put it, "they said I was brainwashed, but I just had to say, 'Well, maybe I am, but let me tell you, it was really dirty![27]'" Clearing out one's mind is the first step in getting control of it.

We let these holy words wash over us, not trying to "get" anything, but simply allowing them to flow, as they become part of us, and we with them. One of the oldest uses, really, for the Holy Writ *is* this "cleansing meditation." We can play a recording of chanted Psalms, though it is far better in the congregation, and silently allow the words to flow. As they become familiar we tend to let them flow over our own lips as well, and better instruct our hearts.

Orthodox Christians, who follow a faith much older, and completely foreign to all that people call, "Christian" in the Modern West, have a form of worship that traces back near 3,500 years. Of course, some details have changed with parts referring to things come to pass since then. Maybe for a couple of hours, sometimes for several, in the light of candles and the smoke of incense, we chant the ancient psalms, hymns, and prayers. Why, chant?

Theatre students study Interpretation. How we say things is often more important than what we say. A different stress on a syllable, or a change of pitch here or there, can completely alter the message people hear, though the words don't change. Singing, especially with instruments behind it, can be even more forceful in getting one's own interpretation across. When something is being read aloud the hearer tends to analyse and second-guess ever word and phrase. Chanting to a set tone keeps any of this from being nearly such an issue. Chanting passes these filters, allows the words simply to *be,* and our spirits simply to *receive.*

As we stand in the sound of the chant, it reaches inside us in ways that an "interpretation" never could. The words themselves – not the reader's delivery, the singer's skill, or even our own impressions – find their places deep within. Songs of hope, despair, and wonder covering thousands of years resonate the very fibre of our souls. A song might appeal to one's right brain and a reading, to the left; a chant reaches the whole person. Like the water for the little lizard, it heals, revives, and renews us.

"We Knew Not Where We Were!"

Something over a thousand years ago, Vladimir, new prince of the *Rus*,[28] wanted a religion to unite his kingdom. He knew that each of his tribes had one that served mainly to support this bunch as better than the other. Was there more to it than that? Some great truth, some common hope or history to keep the peace amongst his chieftains? He sent ten emissaries out to investigate the Religion Question, and bring a report.

They visited a Roman cathedral in Germany, a mosque in Bulgaria, and the Greek cathedral in Constantinople. With the Roman rites and regulations, they had not really been impressed. In Bulgaria, much less so. Of their experience in Greece they said, "We did not know whether we were in Heaven or on Earth!"[29]

What created such awe? First, the Greek cathedral was designed for heart-instruction. As a model of the invisible it marks a coming together of the deepest past and farthest future, Divine and Human, Earth and Heaven, being present to the past and the future, all in one place. But mere symbols, no matter how rich, would not have had that kind of effect. The lights and incense serve as a symbol for the many prayers ascending. The smoke of smoldering tree gum, though, of itself, gives a simple, clean fragrance and the lights are simply from burning olive oil or beeswax. Surely nothing Psychological there. The walls and high-domed ceiling are covered with images of saints and angels with Christ, eternal Tao em-bodied, enthroned above all. But isn't it all just pretty pictures? What caused such fear and awe? One might simply answer, "come and see!" That, in effect, was what the emissaries said.

~§~

A young man once knocked on the monastery gate. The abbot opened.

"I want to see God! How long will it take before I will be able to see God?"

"Oh, is that all you want?" The elder answered. "Well, then, come with me." They passed the beautiful courtyard, then the splendid chapel, through the dining hall. Then the kitchen. Then the scullery, then out back where a gap-toothed old monk, grease and dirt smeared on his wrinkled face, was scrubbing out a scorched pot. "There!"

"What do you mean?" sputtered the guest. "Are you trying to tell me that that old man is God?"

"My son, if you cannot see God in this man, you will never see him anywhere!"[30]

~§~

Breaking the Image

The earliest Christians understood that the Supreme God had made humanity in His image. While some today wonder just what that means, the tradition shows up in the Orthodox Christianity followed in Russia to this day. Some friends who had been in Russia during the Soviet times had heard stories about the *real* Russian army – the *babushkas!* These grandmothers managed, by their prayers and piety, to keep many doors open and candles burning in the remaining Churches through the darkest years. The police respected them, and so did the youth. The police would not bother them at their prayers, and unruly young lads would straighten up when, say, Babushka Irina or Lana would drag her offending grandson by his ears home for supper.

The most striking thing was that, when looking out over the violence and corruption that the state-enforced atheism had brought about it was not uncommon to hear these ladies weep, "They've broken the Image!" If we honor God we honor the Tao, and the inward image of God which is our own tao – our very, inward humanity.[31]

In the West many do not understand this, and even glorify *iconoclasm* – literally, image smashing – as something good and worthy. This comes from the illusion that any kind of religious pictures are "idols," even a picture of Christ in a place dedicated to him. Why would this be?

Many of the earliest Christians were Jewish, and had prayed in their synagogues from childhood. Every one of these was filled with images of all kinds of creatures earthly and heavenly, even in the mosaic floors. The

Hebrew *Torah* forbids disrespect to parents, murder, adultery, theft, covetousness, and idol worship. The same *Instruction* commanded they set reminders of God's mercy in their holy places.

Now, this icon-smashing thing got started when Muslim armies attacked Eastern Christian cities. They tried to demoralise their enemy by telling them that their icons were "gods." [32] (In those days, more than now, people saw Islam as a departure from Christianity.) Beyond that, of course, is the ancient Greek philosophy that everything visible is corrupt, but that's well-covered by better writers.[33]

Gullible mobs[34] started smashing mosaics, painted images, and even such symbols as grapevines and candle stands. What they missed is that, just like having special memories in photographs celebrates those memories, having icons of the Christ and those close to Him celebrates that the Tao really did become Human.

Bear in mind, though, that when we break trust, ultimately, with our own integrity we deny our own tao, the very core of who we are - the divine image inside us. Our inner mob of passions and attachments drives us to think, say, even do unspeakable things, which we often cover up with some justification even like the people of that day convinced themselves they were "doing God a service" by burning Him, as it were, in effigy. With a picture of someone we honor, do we put it in a high place , or under our feet? You and I are holy icons of Heaven. As Zhuang Tse so well put it that there is a Tao of Heaven – that is, from the old Chinese meaning, of the God of Heaven – and a tao of our humanity, which answers to the

Heavenly Tao. What we do with the divine image, our humanity, makes all the difference. When we betray it we violate our divinity as if we hanged it from a tree. Our actual core is the very image of our Source. For all the ways we have desecrated that image, that icon, that tao within us there must be restoration. Not that the Tao is some impersonal force or abstract design, but we are persons, able to think, do, and care, because our tao reflects Heaven. We are not to be clones, at least in the Science Fiction sense of slavish copies, but children of Heaven, and as the Tao is free, and as the wind is free, in such a way must we also fulfill our own purpose in the Tao. When our inner tao is reunited to the Tao of Heaven it finds its destiny. If we abuse the divine image – whether in a person, in nature, or in these icons – we are in fact joining those ignorant mobs, and destroying all that is good within us in effigy, erecting bare walls of our own isolation and despair as icons to glorify, and exalting our own human opinions as the highest power.

Restoring the Image

Since, "that which can be known is not the eternal Tao," if we will find the Tao, it is more by the listening than the studying. How could this be any clearer than if the Tao were born as a fellow human being and lived his lifetime among us, teaching and doing truth? This is just what happened, as one of those who knew this Man wrote, "in the beginning was the Tao, and the Tao was with God, and the Tao was God," and, "the Tao was made flesh, and lived among us... full of *Te* and Truth.[35]" He himself said, "I am the Way (the Tao), the Truth, and the Life." What does this mean, do you think? So, these images mean much more than paint and wood, as I hope this book will be more significant for you than mere paper and ink.

~§~

There is this word again, *Te*. What are we saying? *Te* is the virtue, the energies, by which the Tao guides and maintains all that is made – all of nature, from the harmonics of atomic particles to the dark energies of the universe, including you and me. We might speak of the energies behind natural the energies such as from which flow the fire of the stars, and the weakest nerve impulse. We learn in school that an energy applied is a force. Why do we speak of Te as *energies* and not *forces?* Because, like wisdom, it is useful for all things. When the hub is open, it is useful; when it is applied to a particular axle, then it becomes profitable in that one thing. We might say that Te is not a force because it is not Heaven's plan to force us, but release these energies within.

~§~

While the images of the Tao-Man and His holy ones can be incredibly beautiful[36], they are not for decoration. First of all they remind us that only as the Tao is made Flesh we have a link between Heaven and Earth, Flesh and Spirit. As a Man, he could be seen, touched, and handled, as well as drawn, painted, and – had there been film – photographed. If we even begin to comprehend such an event, how can we not celebrate it? As the eternal Tao lives through all Spirit and of Matter, the Tao-Man comes as one of us to open the door from distant wonderings to such a closeness as to say we live *in* him.

All the universe, and especially humanity, is seeded with splendor, reflecting the divine Creator. Some encounter this through telescopes, some microscopes, some with a brush or a pen, but ultimately with the eyes and ears of our hearts. The Wherever we look, and especially whoever we look at, there is God, and the purer our hearts the better we see. Holy icons demonstrate these two facts – the living bridge, and the inner sight – right to the heart. As one sage wrote that the beauty of God is seen in a human life fulfilled,[37] this fulfilment, this mystery of mastery is what we are about.

How does this apply today?

One thing about using icons in prayer is that they are silent witnesses. They point to a love far greater than our experience can conceive or words express – that the divine Tao would become human, to live our life with us. They speak no words, and no scholars can parse out their grammar; they just are, and call us to just be. Do we need to understand photons, color theory, or eye structure to appreciate a sunset? Yet there was more wisdom in one of these images than many books, and more value than thousands spent on tuition.

So, what do we do with this? First we see it on the basic level of a street sign. While the image on a sign might mean, "Men Working," or, "Curve Ahead," a holy icon is a symbol which stories the work of the Tao. The first thing we see in an icon is a reminder of God at work in our own lives.

Every picture tells a story, and these, more so. There is far more in one of these little panels than could ever fit with words and letters. They aren't "photographic," and don't try to be portraits or news pictures, but color epics. Each part of the panel is one more reminder of some aspect of the person's life, or death. Of the thousands, many many speak in some way of his or her passing – largely because these are the "one in ten" whom death could not touch. They had already embraced theirs.

Also, as we have seen the street-sign-level meaning of the icon, and begun to fathom the depth of the message, we have no reasonable option but to thank God for his "unspeakable gift" given us through the Tao-Man, in whichever saint or event we see represented. One way is that we simply touch our forehead, chest, and right and left shoulders, as to make a Cross on ourselves. This is a physical prayer, asking the blessing of Jesus' Cross be applied to our lives. A kind of moving mudra, if you will. In another way, we bow before our Lord, the Tao, as it is his Te represented in what we see in the icon, and in a third we kiss the icon as a way to express love and relatedness to all that is seen there. Nothing magical, simply common, meaningful motions.

So, then, it is not so much that gazing at a picture will fill one's brain with knowledge, but considering the truths portrayed on that block of wood, that the Unknowable has become Known.

The Work of the People

Once, in a new city, I was looking for a prayer service of the kind as I was accustomed in the commune's tradition – completely impromptu and unrehearsed. I found one in a small church some miles from my base. All there, of course, were strangers to me. I sat around with them as they shared different details of their lives, sang songs together, and prayed. Afterward some of them invited me to come back the next night for an "all saints" prayer service. For lack of a better plan, I went.

All stood. All prayed. All sang. Old hymns, and older prayers, many of them about the company of the holy ones, sages, and miracle-workers of old, who are yet in our midst, though long dead in this eyes of this world. All of them, still with us within the Divine Presence. There was a lesson about how these people assist us even now in our own struggles as we help one another in our prayers. My own Modern opinions drove me for a long time to question all this, to reduce it to psychology, or some other confusion but from that evening my life began to be about stepping into that mystery I had encountered there.

Ancient Christian spirituality occurs in the struggle to acquire the Eternal. To attain the Kingdom of Heaven first we dissolve our attachment to this temporal world – to die to what we call "self," and all power this outward world claims over us. Going back to the monkey, when he no longer grasps the rice in his paw, he is free from the trap; when he no longer desires it in his mind, he is immune to them. Detachment, and dispassion. When we have renounced this world, and no longer desire its attractions, it has dissolved for us. When we embrace our own mortality, and count ourselves as dead to the "illusion," then we have begun to live.

When we stand before the Tao we confront two unknowns. This vastly *Other*, of course, but also another unknown. The Tao, and our own tao – who we are, what we are, our possibilities, and our here-and-now reality. We are not alone. Never have been, never will be. We stand before a great Crevasse of discovery, drawing us ever forward. Do we follow, or back off into the shadow of our own fears?

I kept attending worship, and finding strength, there. It was all nice enough, in itself, but the attraction was much more *inward.* There was definitely something *else.*

Still questioning, I would visit a more Modern church every once in a while for perspective on this new-old discovery. What I noticed was that I was starting to see the other as operating like a high-school pep-rally or an opening band at a rock concert. Is worship about enabling folks to feel after God, or to just feel good? In these gatherings any sense of the Tao at all would lost in the mood music and other distractions. There was no sense of connectedness but isolation. The experience was designed to appeal to the individual, so that each person would be comfortable in his or her own little bubble, with no regard or relation to anybody else in the room. It all seemed to be a matter of how each person was relating to whatever was happening onstage, and the general sense of being there was assumed to be "the Holy Spirit." One has to wonder – do people honestly expect God to need amplifiers and mood music, or be honored from people giving up all self-control, like the crowd at a rock concert or a voodoo rite? Their own Bible says that self-control is evidence that God is active in one's life; why do these churches assume the opposite?

So where is Truth? How do we find the Tao? What does it take to encounter, or be encountered by, God? Lao Tse gave voice to the Tao when he wrote, "My words are easy to understand and easy to perform; yet no one under heaven knows them or practices them.[38]"

The Truth, the Tao, can't be analysed or charted out, but lived, and gained through living. The first step in "finding" the Tao is knowing that the Tao is not to be found, so knowing that much is progress. When we meet the Tao, it is because the Tao has found us, not the other way. The "finding," then, is not in seeking knowledge or power for our own use. Not by grasping with the monkey-fists of our desires, but releasing. No longer demanding, but allowing; not grinding it through our own mental machinery, like with geometry or physics, but the whole heart, soul, strength, and mind – *living* the Tao, ever mindful, dispassionate, and un-attached.

The ancient Chinese tradition, as I have learned so far, is that the people worshiped

Tian, God of the Heavens from before the first dynasty as the One above and beyond all, or *transcendent,* as the scholars would say. So, then, the exaltation of Tian is fulfilled in the lowliness of the Tao. Ancient Christian teaching, from around 80 CE, tells us that "the Tao became flesh" in the person of Jesus Christ, and suffered all the pains that we experience. In this our own suffering is no longer wasted pain, but taken on as part of himself. This goes beyond what this book tries to cover except to say that the unseen, divine mystery is now a Person – like us, but free of despair.

In the ancient Hebrew psalms, the king who would become known as the "Shepherd of Israel" sings that God is his shepherd – not a judge, jailer, or executioner, but shepherd, one who feeds, guides, heals, and protects. We must be mindful of this with so many voices out there making any matter of faith, or spiritual growth a matter of answering to some little army of rule-checkers, and representatives of some cosmic grouch with a fist full of damnation. That is just silly. Those same scriptures speak of wisdom as peaceable, not paranoiac; gentle, not grievous. We learn the ways of Tian, and of the Tao, by setting aside our desires for a greater Good, even knowledge of the Tao, which reveals to us Tian.

These days we find a "detachment" through drugs, or football, or through the religious mood control mentioned earlier. Some detach so completely that the pieces never fit back together, whether from a drug we take or chemistry our own bodies make as we abuse our own emotions, that disorders our minds and destroys our self-control. We don't just need detachment, but dispassion, and mindfulness, in all things. As the sage, Maximos, said, "Dispassion engenders love."

As light banishes darkness, and life, death, so hope is freedom from despair and from the "suffering" of the illusion that this world, this life, is all there is. We set our hopes on what we can see, don't we? A competition runner's hope builds on seeing the tape at the finish line, a sailor's heart is lifted up when he sees his home port coming up on the horizon, and a lover's, at the sight of the beloved. So also our race is set before us to reach the love above all loves, and we have a greater navigator than any harbor master. The Tao is the Road, and Christ, the Tao-Man, is with us through it all.

Now most people who have read the Bible know that God gave Moses the Law, or, Instruction, on Mt. Sinai. Some can even date it around 1440 BCE. Not many will know, though, that he taught them a liturgy, an order of worship, to reflect the ongoing worship in the Heavens.

One of the challenges of writing this book is discussing things which no human being alive can explain, and this is one of them. Is this "in the Heavens" a physical location? Is it a spiritual location? What would a spiritual location look like? All I know is if I claimed to understand it I would be the liar. It could be that our Modern point of view has more to offer, or it could be that Moses had a clue we haven't seen yet, or it could be we are all living on the back of a massive flea.

While we can probably leave the flea out of the picture, we do have a story we can't just toss off so easily. This Liturgy which Moses delivered that day served as a meeting point between God and the Hebrews at their Temple, or, "Place of Meeting," for over a thousand years, and then was adopted by Jesus' Apostles and used by the Orthodox Christian Churches ever since. Even today we have the Liturgy of St. James, and one of St. Andrew, two of Jesus' close followers, and two named for men called Basil the Great and John Chrysostomos, as they wrote down what the Christians had been doing from memory then for hundreds of years. All but Andrew's are really similar, with a different prayer here or there. Andrews' is more specialised.

So what is this all about, one might ask. What profit is there to this liturgy thing, even if it did come from God? Like all of the Instruction, it is an expression of mercy and love. The Commandments, to keep us safe, and the Liturgy to save us.

So, more questions – what do I mean, "safe," and, "save?"

The Commandments were given to keep the people safe. Don't steal, don't mess with your mate's mate, help the poor, and everybody lives a happy life. No feuds, no fights, everything is good. Save? Any way we look at it, it all fits. Psychology talks about restoring inner integrity. All the desires, anxieties, dreams, ambitions; all relationships within oneself, and beyond oneself are in balance. Under control. Safe, as rescue from our own fears, passions, and despair? Got that, too. Ultimately, that our own tao is at one, reconciled, to the Tao of Heaven, at one with Tian.

Lao Tse wrote of the one Tao, the universal Word, Way, and Principle of all that is. Zhuang Tse spoke of a universe full of particular taos – a tao of trees, of elm trees, of this elm, in particular, and likewise for rocks, rivers, stars, and you and me, each corresponding in its way to the Tao of Tian. Confucius wrote of each tao in terms of its purpose, so that a tree is fully *tree* by fulfilling that for which the tree is intended, so the rocks, rivers, stars, &c. No great task, it seems, for a rock or star can only be what it is, and has no distractions – no desires, passions, or distractions to draw it away from being what it is. The earliest Christian writings, such as Paul's letter to the Church at Colossæ,, tell us that the Tao sustains each in its own tao. Confucius in his Analects stressed that a being is only its true self so far as it fulfills its own role and purpose – a king is a king when he acts as a true king, a father, child, or shoe-maker, likewise. A few centuries later, Irenæus wrote that the glory of God is found in a human life fully formed, and we remember Maximos's words, that if we do not fulfill our purpose as human beings – being reconciled with God, we become not less than human, but below all beings which do fulfill their own function in the great design. Some take this as a parallel to Plato's "Doctrine of Forms," which claims that everything on Earth is a reflection of its perfect form in the heavenly realm. What we already do know is that wherever the plans reside, every element of the universe behaves according to its own pattern in ways the human mind cannot fathom.

Every element, that is, except humanity. We read from Paul the Apostle that, "all have *sinned*, and *fall short* of the glory of God," The old Greek language in which he was writing had a word, *amartía*, for *missing the mark*, or being off-target. In England it was translated as *sin* – a common archery term, also, for falling short, or missing the target. All of us monkeys have our hands in some kind of coconut shell, so focused on the scant bit in front of us we lose sight of what life is all about. No surprise there – we attach ourselves to what appeals to our senses, and there we are. We fall short. The prize escapes us because we just lose sight of it. Sure, there is that modern idea of "sin" being about matter of guilt, shame, and how-could-you, but we're not going there. We're on the way, and there's a way to go. We're not yet fully alive, yet, taking part in that *glory,* fulfillment, and ecstasy – *getting beyond ourselves* – that fits it all together.

Zhuang Tse wrote that the masterful person is like the good archer who, when he misses the bullseye, turns around and seeks the reason in himself. More recently, Stephen Mitchell has noted that in turning around this person takes on full responsibility, with no room for blame or denial.[39] The wind was blowing. Was he not in the same wind? The target was far away. Did he not see the distance?

So how does an archer *not* sin? First, by not looking around at all the non-targets. The winning archer isn't concerned with who is in the crowd, what happened the night before, or even his mother's health at that moment. If he is, his shot will be off: he will sin. Curiously, he doesn't stress over hitting the target either.

He goes prepared. Strength-training, breath control, mental focus, and hours of practice. Within his discipline he gives us the model for detachment, dispassion, mindfulness, and the mastery to which these lead. He is where he is, when he is – not where he was or might be later. He is in one moment, in one place. If the arrow is to find its mark, the archer in that moment knows nothing but that one mark. If he compromises his focus, he has compromised his shot. In the military whether something important is sold to the enemy or simply misplaced, it is *compromised*. The archer who compromises his focus *sins*.

To succeed, of course, anything that leads to *sinning* is mindfully kept farthest from the archer's thoughts. These mind weeds must not take root. He will score, and succeed. Is failure impossible? No, but it is not an option. His chosen path is that of an archer, with the disciplines becoming as familiar as breathing and as near and dear as his own heart's beating.

So, getting back to the Liturgy question, what role does it have in *saving* us, in reconciling us to God? It gives us a *form* to shape that transformation and a language to cleanse, and shape our ways of thinking, to prepare for the encounter. So, we become able to channel, and receive, the Te in which it occurs. Ultimately, it is the Tao, and the God of the Tao, whom we encounter through the Te, and who saves us.

Enough of this language, now – what is "saving," anyway? Our own (non) actions – detachment, dispassion, mindfulness – are reflected in three transforming actions of Te: purging us from our attachments and passions for the allure of our senses, illumination to the inward reality, and transformation to the Divine. In fact, if we stay with the electrical picture, our three actions ground us. Any electrical circuit passes from the source through whatever is connected and then to the ground, usually through a long copper stake driven into the earth. If there is no grounding connection, then the current does not flow, and there is no power. Sometimes there is a "false ground," which only allows for a weak flow which ends either when that connection burns up, or our device – motor, light, computer, &c – is destroyed. So, our three non-actions provide the channel for the Te to flow, and for God's three actions to take place. Self-knowledge is essential. Or, as in a dance – He steps forward, we step back; He turns, we follow. As we, He, as He, we, ebb and flow, step by step.

Contemplation

There is a bird you probably know something about, called a nightingale. In Europe and the British Isles it is known and loved for its beautiful singing. It has a cousin in North America which also has a beautiful song, but few ever hear it. This mockingbird picks up the sounds it hears, and repeats them. There can seem to be a cat, crow, or a police siren up in a tree, and, behold, there is that same little grey thrasher. It very much knows how to listen, but gives the most attention to what it hears around it, and not to the natural song within.

There are two more ways God works in us, ways that we are attuned to the Tao, and these are surely the most loving, and the most dangerous. First, there is a method of prayer which traces back, in its most basic form, thousands of years before. At times, this prayer has been attacked by emperors, and those practicing it cast into prison and even executed. In its full development it is shown to be fully Christian and, in fact, basic but, really, key to our growth in the Spirit, but even today there are tirades all over the Internet by people who show they have never spent time looking into what it is, but spend all kinds of time warning people against it.

So, what is so dangerous, that it upsets so many people? Simply being quiet! An ancient prophet once prayed, "Here am I. Send me." A young boy said, "Speak, Lord, your servant is listening." A wise king sang, "Wait on the Lord, be of good courage, and he shall strengthen your heart."

Simply being quiet, though, is as hard a job as anyone can do. If we sit, or stand, for even a minute, before an icon, as discussed, or simply aware of the Divine Presence, simply quiet, our mind rebel, and distract us with every memory, fear, hope, or stray image in reach. In the quiet, with no outer distractions, a person's mind becomes the noisiest place on earth.

The Quiet Way

The Brahmins, long before the time of the Buddha, knew about quietness and detachment. According to one scholar[40], there were some ascetics living on so little that they became like living skeletons. Others went without sleep until their minds were surely at the point of hallucination. Others lay only on beds of sharpened spikes, so they could never relax, even in sleeping.

Young Gautama tried all of these, and more, and he never could escape the distractions of his own mind, much less the "suffering" of being attached to the troubles and desires of this life. After giving up on all the extreme efforts, he sat down under a tree. What happened next gave that species of tree a whole new name. As Gautama sat, he sat longer, and the longer he sat the more he started paying attention to his own breathing. He found that, rather than trying to force himself into some faraway state of being he was able to become mindful of the here and the now, and to become, as he described it, *fully awake.* The tree became known as the Bodhi, or, Wisdom, Tree, as all trees of that species are now called, and Gautama became the Buddha.

Other writers tell us that there were monks using their breathing as part of their meditation long before Gautama, but in their case it seems to be more of using it to force their minds into a particular focus or state. Some more ecstatic religions, whether Pentecostalism or the Dervishes, can be said to alter their states of mind by hyperventilating. The Pentecostal preacher might break up his message into short bursts, with a loud, "hah!" at the end of each, and then a catch-breath and another burst, often for over half an hour, or even hours, with the goal of triggering a similar frenzy amongst the listeners. Dervishes have a similar kind of ecstatic behavior around their "whirling," as I understand. Where there is a spiritual aspect to these customs, the state their breathing brings about surely sets them up to be more receptive as a result. Others, as we have all read or heard about "navel gazing," sit so quietly, and curl themselves inward in such a way, that their breathing rate slows way down. Again, whatever the spiritual dimension, slowing the body's rhythms, and reducing the oxygen going to the brain, is going to have a serious calming effect. In either way, if our aim is a spiritual "marriage" to the Divine, how does self-manipulation move us any closer?

The Buddha's discovery takes us a step closer. Some hyper-focus themselves by hyperventilating; others drop into more kind of a dream state through oxygen starvation. By simply minding his breath as it passed in and out of his body he discovered a sharpened sense of mindfulness which, when others learned it, became a whole new philosophy.[41]

In 2004, the University of Wisconsin cooperated with the Shechen monastery in Kathmandu to do a neural study[42] on a group of Buddhist monks while they were meditating, and when at rest. A group of incoming college students were brought in as "controls" for comparison. To show the potential for the Buddha's philosophy, they compared the gamma-wave activity of the two groups' brains. The lowest level shown by one of the monks was twice the highest shown by the students, and the highest-reading monk was nearly fifteen times higher than the control. This gives us a glimpse of the potential for this most basic step in the "process" here, and while the mindfulness the Buddha teaches is of being more aware of one's own thoughts, there is a mastery that reaches far beyond what any "psychics" dare to boast[43].

Let's jump ahead for a moment. While these techniques bring us to be more aware of the thoughts in our own heads, a number of writers have come out saying that we really can't say that all the thoughts in our heads started off there. There are entities in the spiritual realm: some friendly, and some not. The unfriendlies may inject ideas, but more often they simply dredge up old thoughts we'd rather leave forgotten. Just being mindful to our thoughts without mastering them can lead to all kinds of trouble.

There is an old fable from Æsop about a hungry crow, sitting on a branch hoping for some breakfast. The only candidate he saw was a long centipede. A nice meal, to be sure, but something that long would be a lot of trouble getting into his beak.

> "Hello there, Mr. Caterpillar," he called.

> "Hello yourself, Mr. Crow, and a good morning to you!"

"Yes, indeed! But tell me, please, this one thing I have been wondering for ever so long."

"And what might that be?"

"Well, it's a deep mystery to me, being but a bird, you see, but surely no challenge to yourself. Tell me, friend, when you get out of your bed in the morning, and start off on your walking, just which of those fine feet of yours do you set out first?"

"Well," he began, "that is quite simple, for you see first I set out the first left, and then the forty-second right, and then – oh, that's not right – next comes forty-seven left, and then – oh, that's wrong too..!"

And so he began to demonstrate this, and then try that, and then assay the other, until he

> was soon so tangled up in
>
> himself that in a swoop
>
> and a gulp, the crow had
>
> his breakfast!

And so, odd, but true – if we keep our minds on ourselves, with our own wants, desires, and ambitions, we become like that silly caterpillar: wrapped up in ourselves, and too nearsighted to see even the immediate dangers. We focus on "me," and open ourselves up to the unfriendlies.

Some meditation forms involve repeating a *mantra* over and over as a "centering" technique. This *mantra* is often the name of one of the lesser Hindu gods. Not friendly. Religions which prosper by enslaving children and putting women out for ritual prostitution don't impress me as being all that benevolent, and we do tend to resemble that which we worship, don't we? Even so, when devotion to these gods leads to such acts, then it is safe to say that this does not help us in our spiritual progress. Repeatedly calling on their names while emptying and opening our consciousnesses does not occur as the best idea.[44] There are malevolent entities out there, and benevolent entities. We can call them ME's and BE's.

Now if you will forgive me for using such a lame "chalk talk" illustration, what the *BE's*, and a spiritually healthy life, are about is pretty well wrapped up in a short excerpt from Jesus' teachings called the "Beatitudes." If we would rather have their help than not, it's a good idea to give them as much to work with as we can. Yes, the illustration is weak, but it's a good way to remember things. At the time he first started teaching, the Christ opened up a lesson to his disciples with these words.

Blessed are the poor in spirit: for theirs is the kingdom of heaven.

Blessed are they that mourn: for they shall be comforted.

Blessed are the meek: for they shall inherit the earth.

~

Blessed are they which do hunger and thirst after righteousness:

for they shall be filled.

Blessed are the merciful: for they shall obtain mercy.

Blessed are the pure in heart: for they shall see God.

~

Blessed are the peacemakers: for they shall be called the children of God.

Blessed are they which are persecuted for righteousness' sake:

for theirs is the kingdom of heaven.

Blessed are ye, when men shall revile you, and persecute you, and shall say all manner of evil against you falsely, for my sake. Rejoice, and be exceeding glad: for great is your reward in heaven: for so persecuted they the prophets which were before you. [45]

Three triads of blessedness, three three-part steps, in the progress of "detachment, dispassion, and mindfulness," as we become perfect in love. The first three follow the detachment, dispassion, mindfulness from a beginning, detached, stage; the second is an active denial of the passions for a greater goal; the third follows those same three steps with a greater joy and purpose, even to the point of joyfully enduring even a violent death.

In the first, we begin as "poor in spirit." All that really matters in us is in us. The house I mentioned before? It served its purpose. The family? Children grow up in their own way, and, sadly, sometimes relationships do too. The motorcycle served me well, though I never could find a good machinist for some of the finer engine work. As long as I held onto those things as if they were who I was, I myself as just the shell, the can, and not the crab, with only a clue that there was much more to the crab within than the ability to carry the can.

Step One then is being "poor in spirit:" Anything we have attached to ourselves, or anything that has been attached from outside us is not ourselves, but attachments: possessions, relationships, accomplishments, ancestry, affiliation, beliefs and opinions, etc. When all that is set aside, what is left? Anything we can grasp, anything we can attach to, is not us, is it? We love *with* our hearts, but we hope not many would say they love their hearts; that would be disordered. All any of us is is what we are, and not what we get attached to. Even what we are we hold in open hands. Detaching ourselves from so little, we stand to receive more that our imaginations can conceive.

"Blessed are they that mourn:" we not only recognise that we aren't all that much, in ourselves, but what there is, or what we've done with it, is really pretty bad. We set out to do good for people, but wind up hurting them just from being selfish, shortsighted, or just plain stupid. We resolve to be more honest, more loving, or even more healthy, and that resolution hardly ever survives the first week. We're human, and human beings mess things up. It's just who we are. Without attaching to false identities, we come to honestly hate being like we so easily tend to be, and we begin to have an honest dispassion – a real rejection of our desires for all that distracts us. Mind, it's not a matter of hating the thing, or the relationship, itself, but choosing not to let our desire for it manipulate us!

"Blessed are the meek." Meek is not a whipped puppy, but a trained horse: real power, with real grace. In concert with its master it can do what it would never have dreamed to do otherwise. When the Tao is painted, the strength of the Yang side relies on the core of Yin softness, and the Yin is not complete without the seed of the Yang within. This strength, itself, is not our own, but it is the Te. If, of course, we are speaking of the Tao of Heaven, then this Te is the Te of that Tao. There is also a tao of you or me, and the grace and virtue which it expresses in our lives as we cooperate with the Tao. And the Te of Heaven is not a mere feeling or sensation, as some might imagine, for it guides, heals, and sustains the universe. The early Christians called this, *kharis*, or, *grace*, but in the West grace has come to mean nothing more than, in effect, God saying, "You stink, but I choose to like you to show how good I am." Rather than deal further with this, we'll just keep using *Te*. As we learn to live in yoke with the *Christ/Tao* we become partnered with Him in this work of transformation, and in all He is, knows, and has. This is the transformation; this is the prayer.

We can go on, and touch on the other two triads, but that would take us a little off-course for this book. After all, when somebody has really embodied the first, and even knows about the other two, they do tend to follow.

Love brings us out of ourselves. It relaxes our grip on our own treasures, frees us from selfish passions, and shifts our focus *othersward*. This is one more reason we can't stop with the Buddhist model. A Buddhist's breathing techniques may bring her to be more aware of the thoughts in her mind, and a Zen monk may even fade them all into the background as he reaches a state of "non-being." Each is alone. It is one thing to sit alone and generate compassionate feelings towards Humankind, or all beings; it is another to love them, personally. One English poet I read in school wrote beautiful verse about the Humanity, and would leap into the bushes not to actually meet another person on the road. "I love mankind; it's people I can't stand," as someone said.

So, how do we get outside ourselves? Do we wait until "love" pays a visit, say, in the form of a mind-shattering romance? Who hasn't seen those silly "waiting for Mr. Right" pictures of a skeleton in a fancy dress, sitting on a park bench? What is the most important thing? When asked this, the Christ answered, "to love ..God with all your heart, mind, soul, and strength," and, "to love your neighbor as yourself." What is love, if not mindfulness? As an artist sketches his subject, he learns the details of the face, say, and the ways the light reflects here, shadows there, and brings out different aspects of the personality. He comes to identify with that person, and becomes all the more committed to that picture coming out as the best portrait possible of who he sees. The attention becomes mindfulness, and the mindfulness, a sense of love, or the portrait comes out more as lines and shades – a drafting exercise.[46]

I mentioned "Tao/Christ" earlier. In the English Bible translations St John's Gospel begins with, "in the beginning was the Word, and the Word was with God, and the Word was God; the same was in the beginning with God." Farther in he says, and spends the rest of the book showing, that this "Word" is Jesus Christ. This "Word," in the Greek source text, is, "Logos." and, of course, the Chinese translations use the word, "Tao." "In the beginning was the Tao," etc. Gia-Fu Feng does not seem to have been a Christian in any way I have found, but was more an aging beatnik, and father figure to the hippies. His translation of the Tao Te Ching, though, shows that holy book to be possibly the nearest parallel in the world to the Christian New Testament: the one discusses the invisible and unknowable Tao; the other the revealed Logos. Same word, different languages.

There is a method of prayer – directed meditation – in the Christian tradition that has been around longer than there has been a New Testament.

The goal is the effect, and not simply checking off a list of steps and stages. While we can never reach absolute mastery, perfection, or deification in this life, there is no law about how close we can get. In such a way, Suzuki-Roshi is correct – the goal is the journey, and the journey is the goal.

If we have an *icon*, a painted *image* – of Christ, His mother, one of the saints and sages who have marked this path before us, then we begin by looking briefly at it. We don't fixate on it; we acknowledge that the icon is there and that, in some way so the one(s) represented. We light a candle or oil lamp before the icon as a symbol of our prayer, and of the light which we seek. We might also burn some incense, also to "show" our prayers; frankincense-based kinds, that go on a charcoal, are best. Many of the stick and cone varieties tend to be kind of distracting – kind of like smelling a cake, or a waft of perfume while trying to meditate. "Symbol," is the language of the heart, though a lot of our hearts need to improve their vocabularies.

We light the lamp, we set some incense on the charcoal, and we look briefly at the icon. We are not alone. We might pray such words as, "O Lord, help!"

Or,

> May You be a bright flame before me
> May You be a guiding star above me,
> May You be a smooth path below me,
> And a loving Guide behind me,
> Today, tonight, and forever.
> God be with me in every pass,
> Jesus be with me on every hill,
> Spirit be with me on every stream,
> Headland and ridge and lawn;
> Each sea and land, each moor and meadow,
> Each lying down, each rising up,
> In the trough of the waves,
> on the crest of the billows,
> Each step of the journey thou goest."

While there are many advantages to keeping to the same words, there are also advantages to keeping the same diet. Years ago at college I really liked a light meal of French bread and instant black coffee. By the time, though, that I had finished off the loaves in my dorm room I had a different opinion of both. We don't pray just for the rhythm, or to propel ourselves into some other state of mind. We pray for effect, and for connection. To enroll our hearts we sound the words slowly, deliberately, mindful of just what each phrase means, and what it implies. For the connection, we keep our minds not on the words alone, but to Whom we are ultimately speaking.

There are just three things we need to mind. One is to make the prayer as regular as our breath; the second is to keep our minds on Whom we're addressing. The third is that we find a "soul friend" to advise us as we learn and progress, and warn us of dangers and delusions.

The Soul Friend

A dear friend of mine holds a Ph. D. in Psychology, and has had careers both in practice and as a professor. She knows her field. We were talking one day about the work of the Soul Friend, and a book I had just read about that spiritual art. I mentioned that it had struck me that the 7th century writer understood the human mind as well as or better, than, the modern science offers. She paused, and thought over all she had learned, done, and taught, and said, "you know, I think you're right!"

There are all kind of therapists to help folks feel better about life, break a habit, or get coaching for some interest or another. Nice enough, but none of this really deals with who the person is, or needs to be. Therapists are good. What we need is a Soul Friend.

A Soul Friend is somebody who listens, and guides; who helps us to sort ourselves, to do the kind of cultivation that we wouldn't be able to do without a wise friend's perspective. I use the word, "Soul friend" because it's about the relationship. It translates from the old Gaelic, *anam chara,* as the Celtic monks learned the practice from Egyptian Desert Fathers back during the days when Myrddin and Arthur were in Wales. The idea was not just to have better attitudes or be more creative or vulnerable, to "feel better." An *anam chara* is committed to seeing you *be* better. Each of us is born with the image of God within us; the Soul Friend is there to see it come forth. We are created for intimate, transforming, connection with God; the Anam Chara is qualified and committed to walking with us and guiding us along on just that journey. You don't tell this person, "Bless me, Father for I have sinned," or hear, "We are making progress but the time is up; please pay Francine on the way out."

As You Have Done...

There is an old story of a miserable old woman who, despite her mean habits, had some faithful friends praying for her. The night finally came that she died. From all her selfishness, for all the coldness of her heart, the die was cast, and so she found herself in the midst of Hellish suffering, waist-deep in flaming filth and corruption. Her friends, though, would not cease praying for her, and eventually there came a holy angel, carrying an onion.

He called her by name, and she looked up. "Your friends have been insisting that you be saved, and so we have searched all through your life for some way in which you have cooperated with God's grace, and we found this onion. Do you remember this onion, dear one?" She looked at the onion, and looked hard at it. It was hardly a proper onion at all, but the top was dried and wilted, and the bulb was shiny with decay. Her salvation was related to this. . ? Then she remembered. She had been making a soup, and the first onion out of her bin had looked so bad she decided not to even trim it. As she was on the way to toss it on the pile an old woman appeared at the door, begging a morsel. She had given her that slimy old onion, and gone back to her stew. "This onion cured that old beggar woman of a cold that would have killed her. That was the one deed of mercy we found in your life. So, if you will hold on to this onion I will pull you out of the pit and carry you to Paradise."

Overjoyed, she grabbed the old vegetable with both hands. As she started to rise out of the pit, desperate souls all around her crowded in, some grabbing her skirts and ankles, some scrambling for a hold on the onion. She immediately started struggling and kicking at them. "Get away! Let go! This is my onion!" Immediately, it fell apart, and she fell hopelessly back into the misery.

While this story well appears made-up, it tells us of an ancient principle that what good we manage to do in this life is counted before God on a scale that far outweighs our expectation. If an investor had a promise of a thousand-fold increase, would he be content to buy a dollar's worth of this stock, or would he be wise to sell out whatever he could to invest all the more? And what if the return were not mere currency for this life, but the very love of God active and alive in his life forever? Many who get a glimpse of this "return on investment?" become known by a new name: *holy fools*. A widow in 18th c. St. Petersburg sold off all her possessions, gave the money to the poor and the Church, and lived her last forty-five years on the streets in her late husband's military uniform, and begging money and building materials for a new Church building.

There was also a nun in Paris, shortly after the Bolshevik revolution in Russia. There were huge numbers of homeless women among the refugees, and she sought out all she could, opening her home to them. And another home, and another, as the needs arose. Though a nun, she would often be out in the city during prayer times searching the streets and back-alleys where these poor women would be hiding. Public opinion didn't even register with her; people could plainly see she was a nun, but if she was hot and thirsty while in town she thought nothing of stopping at a bistro for a beer and a cigarette. She was about seeing God in others much more than herself being seen as anything. In fact, when her bishop suggested she become a nun, she protested. "I can't be a good nun!" "No, you can't," the wise man answered, "I want you to be a *revolutionary* nun!" She put on the simple black dress and head-scarf of a Russian nun, and lived the rest of her life in revolutionary compassion for others.

This last method is at the end for its own reason. Without it, some of us might not get out of our chairs, but fold ourselves up inside ourselves, seeking our own inner silence. While we might have seven different ways of drawing close to God, or opening to Him, in the quiet of our own homes, this eighth way is a new beginning to make sure we don't stop short!

The Dakota people understood, "'The longest road you're going to have to walk is from here to here. From your head to your heart." This is the road we are on; this is the path we all must travel.

St. Gregory of Nyssa wrote, "This is the safest way to protect the good thing you enjoy: by realising how much your Creator has honored you above all others creatures. He did not make the heavens in His image, nor the moon, nor the sun, nor the beauty of all the stars, nor anything else which surpasses all understanding. You alone are an icon of Eternal beauty, and if you look at Him you will become as He is, imitating Him Who shines within you, Whose glory is reflected in your purity. Nothing in all creation can equal your grandeur. All the heavens can fit in the palm of God's hand. . . and though He is so great, . .you can wholly embrace Him. He dwells within you. . . He pervades your entire being."

Beginning

My dear reader, dear friend, thank you for walking with me through this sorting-out exercise. In this short book we have unpacked concepts and practices which, as many people as have shared them over the ages, so many have been divided over the exact things they have all actually shared. Why are cats like they are, or ivy vines? Did Nature develop them? Did the Universe? The Tao, the Logos? What is your own name? Is it, or is that just an agreed-upon set of sounds you've been trained to look up when you hear it? Life is full of foolish questions, isn't it?

Yet, I have tried to share that which can't be spoken. I have done this willingly, and I beg your forgiveness. True transformation, true divinisation, is not actually the path we must walk, but is encountered on the path – an experience that can be discussed, but never taught. This book serves only to offer directions for finding, and following, that path. Illumination is found in walking it, not merely discussing the route. Though the ancient Paul had gained the purity to heal the sick and even revive the dead and survive a stoning he wrote, "I count not myself to have attained." I have far more ground to cover than he, Zhuang Tse, or many others, so please do not think to follow me, or imagine I would make such an invitation, or the journey would be very short, but walk with me on the path that is the Tao, the Logos, the Christ Himself. Yes, and I do hope I have made it clear that this path, being seen clearly in the converging paths – in the ways of the Buddha, in the Zen tradition, and in the Tao, as they all give way to the ancient truth of the earliest Christians – is very different from the silly battleground between the Fundamentalists and the Modernists. Truly, they are all entirely Modern and the path cannot be traveled simply by holding onto this or that hallowed opinion anymore than by holding onto a rabbit's foot or clover leaf.

When you began this book, it was probably more for curiosity. "What does this person have to say," or, "Is there something I can use?" Now, you have been through these discussions, and you are still reading. You see that this whole matter is not a mere "self improvement" course, like a trip to an, "insight spa." Yes, those are useful, for what they do. This is not a matter, though, of getting a little wiser, or looking better to oneself, but becoming truly alive and completely human, through our lives becoming fully involved in God, and He, in us. No weekend seminar, no casual reading, or insight session: Life itself. Please do read this book again, and consider how you might best use what I have shared in your own life.

Lao Tse also wrote, "Where the Mystery is the deepest is the gate of all that is subtle and wonderful." Let's move on, then, into the Mystery.

> We shall not cease from exploration
>
> And the end of all our exploring
>
> Will be to arrive where we started
>
> And know the place for the first time.
>
> T.S. Eliot[47]

Acknowledgments

My thanks first of all for vital help and encouragement go, first of all, to my amazing wife, Dr. Kristina Knutson. This book would not be here without her support and insights. I cannot imagine a better travel companion in this journey than she.

A dear friend and student in China, who would, I think, rather not be named, is owed every gratitude for her own support and encouragement. She knows who she is, and graciously holds my debt in open hands.

To Dr. Katharine Clark, your insights both from History and Psychology have been a greater help than you'll ever know.

I must also acknowledge two Kenyan friends, Dr. Reuben Langa'at, and the Rev'd Arthur Toro. They taught me, among other things, two vital lessons of African philosophy. One of these is, "Slowly by slowly." A task worth doing deserves the patience to finish it. The other, "I am because we are," reminds us we are all in this together, and none of us lives to himself if he lives at all. Reuben and Arthur, mheshimiwa sana!

Thanks, also, to the various gurus, priests, and scholars who have contributed by their own teaching, writing, and suggestions. , and combing my manuscripts for errors. I'll spare you the notoriety by not mentioning you by name, but you know who you are, and I love you!

Finally, grateful acknowledgement to my onetime coach, Elissa Conklin, and the members of the Gwinnett County Writers' Guild. I am because we are!

Closing notes:

This book is, decidedly, non-fiction. No names have been changed, and none of its accounts made-up or embellished. Some of its stories may seem unusual, but no more so than a rogue wave at sea may challenge the *common sense* of one who has always lived inland or the splendors of the night sky, one accustomed to a brightly lit city. A brilliant lecture I once attended opened with the instructor making a small dot on a large circle on a chalk board. "This dot," he said, , "represents all that we know we know." A thin wedge was "what we know that we don't know. The big circle itself? "This is what we don't know that we don't know." I hope I have been able to draw the readers' attention to the universe beyond the circle.

Further Reading:

Here are some books I'd like to recommend from my own reading. Some of them I have in electronic formats which don't have the full author/date/publisher info. In in no particular order, though, here are some good ones.

First off, Gia-Fu Feng and Jane English produced an illustrated translation of the *Tao Te Ching* which is well worth looking up. I searched through several translations before finding this one. It presents the Tao as a Unity rather than trying to present each verse as a poem in itself, and the work flows as subtly as a quiet stream.

Taoism: The Ultimate Collected works of 23 Essential Books and Texts seems to be available only as a download. The biblio data don't seem to appear. It is as the title claims a great reference with writings from many of the Chinese masters.

Similarly, an old book entitled *Sacred Books of the East*, compiled by Epiphanius Wilson, George Sale, James Darmesteter, Samuel Beal, and F. Max Müller offers a selection including the Vedic Hymns, Dhammapada, and the Life of the Buddha. For reference or contemplation, it's a good resource.

The Druids: The History and Mystery of the Ancient Celtic Priests by Jesse Harasta from Charles River Editors gives us a glimpse into one of the world's least understood religious traditions. My cap is off to this young professor for his dedication.

Lady Gregory, of "Irish Renaissance" fame and friend of W. B. Yeats, was a grand example of both artistry and scholarship, not least of her works being *Gods and Fighting Men: The Story of the Tuatha de Danaan and of the Fianna of Ireland.* While I don't draw from her book here, she provided a great resource into the study of religious history.

The Art of War by Sun Tse (or Tzu…) is a great insight into the mind of the ancient Chinese dynasties. At one time Sun Tse killed an emperor's favorite wife for failing to properly command a practice platoon of palace women as part of a "job interview" as commander of the guard. He got the job.

The Book of the Dead gives us a glimpse of the ancient Egyptian pantheon, its origins, and the people's view of them. Most of all, it shows part of the overall theme of the earliest "insights" to the nature of the Tao.

Herlee Creel has a book out, *Chinese Thought; From Confucius to Mao Tse Tung,* which tries to lay out a philosophical history of the Chinese people. It would take me decades to be expert enough to say how well he did with it, but it is a good read, and it lays things out in an orderly fashion, which I appreciate.

One more anthology, *Philosophies of India*, by Heinrich Zimmer and edited by Joseph Campbell, is a wonderful resource. I first found it in a friend's friend's stacks, and held onto it until he was demanding it back before I found a copy in the stores.

Moving to more recent works, Aldous Huxley wrote a book called *The Perennial Philosophy* which lays out details of how the various religious traditions have more in common than mere theft or coincidence can account for. It's always good to find one's own "discoveries" showing up from so many years earlier, and from a writer as well-beloved as Mr. Huxley!

Along that line, anthropologist Donald Richardson started off as a Baptist missionary to Southeast Asia There he discovered that the popular story about religion starting with a primitive fear of lightning and "evolving" into more elaborate myths is really its own myth. His first book, *Eternity in Their Hearts,* challenges much of what we "know" on this topic, and is well worth the read regardless one's persuasion.

Edward Slingerland's *Trying Not to Try* brings the inner art of Zhuang Tse's Wu Wei philosophy into terms we in the Modern West can take hold of. He combines insights from Zhuang Tse, Lao Tse, Mencius, and current Neuroscience to present Effortless Progress to a stressed and pressured society. A very good read!

Chinese History prof Michael Puett and author Christine Gross-Loh combine their talents on *The Path; What Chinese Philosophers Can Teach Us About the Good Life.* This is based from Dr. Puett's highly popular Harvard course in Chinese thought, and offers us more insights into Wu Wei and how to apply them in our daily lives.

Along this line, Stephen Mitchell's book, *The Second Book of the Tao,* combines the teachings of Lao Tse and his disciple Zhuang Tse into a delightful collection of 64 chapters which brings their teachings into a focus easy for the Modern reader to appreciate. Mitchell is one of the true scholars in his field, and an elegant writer.

John O'Donahue's *Anam Cara; A Book of Celtic Wisdom* gives a poetically written insight into what a Soul Friend really is as well as the intrinsic holiness – the, "otherness" - of the world around us. Though, officially, the man is an Irish Catholic priest many of his insights appear as remarkably Buddhist. A calming, thoughtful read.

Some years before becoming an Orthodox Christian abbot, or a Christian, Eugene Rose discovered the Tao. He was so deeply effected that he studied Ancient Chinese to be able to help his favorite grad-school professor create a new translation of the Tao Te Ching. Once he became a monk he began work on his *Christ the Eternal Tao* which his successor Damascene Christenson would complete after his untimely death. The "C word" in the title may skew its readership somewhat, but it is a good read for all backgrounds – especially the first chapters.

Zhuang Tse, or, "Zhuangzi or Chuang Tse, as other spell it, penned what we know as the "Inner Chapters" seen as crucial to understanding Philosphical Taoism. (There are "outer chapters" and "mixed chapters," penned by his disciples and later followers, respectively.) Gia-Fu Feng and Jane English released *Chuang Tsu Inner Chapters, A New Translation* in 1974 which shows this stunning work to be one of the world's great examples of Wisdom Literature. My own copy resides on the top of my bedside bookshelves.

Chop Wood, Carry Water is a Western classic in the Eastern tradition. With a view to the spirituality of the everyday, its collection of stories and essays helps the reader connect with the sacred aspects of relationships, work, sex, money, technology, and more. It is not so much the fruit of an author's or editor's effort, but the shared effort of a team of writers related to the New Age Journal. As such, it reads much like a magazine complete with engaging photos, with a depth the reader will appreciate.

Zen Mind, Beginner's Mind is a collection of talks from Zen Master Shunru Suzuki, and probably the most influential American book in that tradition[48]. Opening it to a favorite line I read, "Our way is not to sit (zazen) to acquire something; it is to express our true nature. That is our practice." This is the Zen way. It is the "one hand clapping," which makes no sound, but is heard everywhere at once.

Harvard Psychologist Richard Alpert went to India with a pocketful of LSD tabs to further his studies in the nature of spirituality. Baba Ram Dass returned with a new perspective and the notes for his book, *Be Here Now*. This book outlines his journey, his own discovery of Yoga, and a catalogue of ideas, methods, and resources for creating an intentionally spiritual lifestyle. Along with Zen Mind, Beginner's

Mind it became the starting point for millions on the path to a new level of discovery. It was also the inspiration for the style of my own little book here, and I hope I have done it justice.

Finally, The Routledge Dictionary of Gods, Goddesses, Devils, and Demons has been an immense help as I discovered the parallels amongst the various ancient traditions. The same concepts, and the same personalities, occur in civilisations all over the world. The main differences are the names, and even so the meanings behind those names differ mainly by the languages that created them. The American Indian "Sky Father" corresponds with the Chinese "High One of the Heavens" and the Hebrew "Exalted One(s)." It is not that often one is so intrigued by a naming catalogue.

And Now, the End Notes:

[1] Some writers approach anything historical that is morally uplifting with an implacable suspicion. Sorry for them, but we have what we have, and while they are welcome to show their rationale for doubting the historical record they are also responsible for dealing with the reasons for accepting it.

[2] The Modern Chinese seems to limit *Te* to human acts of virtue, which would be hard-pressed to fit this ancient context.

[3] On the other hand, lots of textual scholars spend their days dealing with matters that seem to belong more in the realm of archæology than the sense of the text, so who knows?

[4] It is an interesting thing that while Christians think of the Divine Spirit in terms

[7] Archimandrite Tikhon (Shevkunov). *Everyday Saints and Other Stories*. Translation by Julian Henry Lowenfeld. Pokrov Publications, 2012.

[8] This hermit-monk is known as St. Seraphim of Sarov. More can be found about him in *Holy Joy: The Heartbeat of Faith* by Anthony M. Coniaris and *St. Seraphim of Sarov: An Icon of Orthodox Spirituality* by Paul Evdokimov

[9] According to the then-popular "Don Juan" books by Carlos Castaneda, eating psychedelic plants in their natural environment would allow a person to receive a visit from his spirit guide, which would appear as some kind of magical animal, ideally the likes of a white crow, and

border, he later could never prove such a man existed, and his "Native wisdom" was more in line with the Oriental philosophies popular in that day than anything taught by Native Americans.

[10] These names are *not* changed in hope they will get back in touch.

[11] During that time every city and county seat had an office staffed with a few clerks handling the administrative side of drafting young men into the military. This would range from processing eligibility status to issuing arrest warrants for non-compliance.

[12] What we "know," before we start thinking, can be called "first principles." If one knows his country to be the greatest in the world,

mastery of seas in bamboo boats, or understanding the reindeer.

[13] This is not a book of comparative theology, so I will be forced to leave the interpretive particulars in the realm of mystery.

[14] Shunryu Suzuki, *Zen Mind, Beginner's Mind*, 2000, Weatherhill, New York

[15] Richardson, Donald: *Eternity in their Hearts*, Regal Books, Ventura, 1981

[16] For what it's worth, nobody seems to know how many writers are represented, especially when much of it is court records and histories covering hundreds of years in a single document.

[17] From a talk by Fr. Thomas Hopko, late Dean Emeritus, St. Vladimir's Orthodox Theological Seminary, Crestwood, NY.

[18] Philokalia, v. 1, pp. 62-63, text 71

so seeks to be filled with the divine presence through breath prayer, and the other practices presented in this small book rather than cultivating long silences.

[20] "It is better to be unhappy and know the worst, than to be happy in a fool's paradise." Fyodor Dostoyevsky. The Idiot. Methuen, London: 1971

[21] My "master's" degree serves me only to realise how much I need to grow and to learn – that I am but a simple student saying, "come learn with me!"

[22] Bernard of Chartres, some 5 ½ centuries before, had written, "..we are like dwarves perched on the shoulders of giants, and thus we are able to see more and farther than the latter. And this is not at all because

[24] C. S. Lewis, "The Dark Island." The Chronicles of Narnia, 5. *The Voyage of the Dawn Treader.* HarperCollins New York:, 1980.

[25] Maximos the Confessor, ca. 580-662, Constantinople.

[26] Basil the Great, ca. 329-379 CE, Cæsaræa

[27] Overheard in conversation, around 1970

[28] Prince Vladimir of Kyiv, in the late 10th century, CE

[29] When we journeyed among the Bulgars, we beheld how they worship in their temple, called a mosque, while they stand ungirt. The Bulgarian bows, sits down, looks hither and thither like one possessed, and there is no happiness among them, but instead only

whether we were in heaven or on earth. For on earth there is no such splendour or such beauty, and we are at a loss how to describe it. We know only that God dwells there among men, and their service is fairer than the ceremonies of other nations. For we cannot forget that beauty. Every man, after tasting something sweet, is afterward unwilling to accept that which is bitter, and therefore we cannot dwell longer here." Then the vassals spoke and said, "If the Greek faith were evil, it would not have been adopted by your grandmother Olga, who was wiser than all other men." Vladimir then inquired where they should all accept baptism, and they replied that the decision rested with him. *The Russian Primary Chronicle:*. Cambridge, Mass.: Mediaeval Academy of America, 1953

[30] From a talk by Rev. Dr. Thos. Hopko, Dean Emeritus, St. Vladimir's Orthodox Theological Seminary.

[31] Aleksandr I. Solzhenitsyn, "Paradigms and Demographics." *: Foreword to The Socialist Phenomenon by Igor Shafarevich*. N.p., n.d. Web. 21 Apr. 2015. q.v.

[32] An interesting thing about this dogma is that it came from Islam. When we look at the various traditions which follow it today, we see other Islamic characteristics have developed. Islam, remember, means "submission," Christians who use icons

don't just "submits," but worship with an outward expression of their faith. The sects most strict about condemning icons compensate by finding ways to enforce a submission to their particular ideologies. They exalt their "Prophet(s)," devalue women, prohibit certain meat and drink, &c.

[33] Freeman, Stephen, *Everywhere Present*, Conciliar Press, 2012, St. John Damascene, *Three Treatises on the Divine Images*, ca. 726 CE

[34] When have we had discerning mobs?

[35] Paraphrased from John's Gospel in the New Testament, chap. 1, from the Chinese translation

[36] In, *The Idiot*, Fyodor Dostoyevsky writes, "The prince says that the world will be saved by beauty! And I maintain that the reason he has such playful ideas is that he is in love." Yet, if we give up on our playfulness today, what is left in the

morning?

[37] "The glory of God is a living man; and the life of man consists in beholding God," St Ireneaus, *Against Heresies*, IV 20:7, ca. AD 180

[38] *Tao Te Ching*, ch. 70

[39] Mitchell, Stephen, *The Second Book of the Tao,* Penguin Press, 2009, New York

[40] Mark Muesse, Associate Professor of Religion, Rhodes College, in a lecture series,"Religions of the Axial Age," Great Courses, Course # 6312

[41] Religion-wise, Buddhism seems to stay within the greater Hindu tradition. Though the Buddha is quoted as saying, "if you find God, kill him," many Buddhists today follow the Hindu tradition of worshipping one of the many gods as one facet, and the personification of one God which is expressed in all of them. Zen

Buddhism, possibly the most pure and original sect of his teachings, distills this to, "if you find the Buddha, kill him," each person becoming Buddha.

[42] "Long-Term Meditators Self-Induce High-Amplitude Gamma Synchrony During Mental Practice," *Proceedings of the National Academy of the Sciences of the United States of America,* vol. 101, no. 46

[43] On the other hand, in the book, *The Buddha pill: can meditation actually change you?* London: Watkins, 2015. author Miguel Farris tells of cases in which Buddhist-style meditation has led to manic episodes, messianic delusions, and even suicidal ideation.

[44] For a number of examples, please read, (Dionysios Farasiotis, and Alexis Trader) *The Gurus, the Young Man, and Elder Paisios.* Platina, CA: St. Herman of

Alaska Brotherhood, 2008.

[45] "The Beatitudes," Matthew 5:3-12, as presented in the Authorised Version of the Holy Bible, rev. 1789 revision, Cambridge.

[46] This can be seen in the way in which, say, "The Girl with the Pearl Earring" or many other portraits reflect a kind of glow far beyond mere technical skill, or the inward sensation of focusing on one's subject while making even a simple sketch. Josef Karsh was a view-camera photographer for the big news magazines in the mid-20th century. Before shooting a celebrity, be it Winston Churchill or Audrey Hepburn, he would research his subject, and his subject's hobbies and passions, to discuss them with his subjects at the shoot. The sense of mindful love he experienced toward each of them gives a glow to the pictures over and above his meticulous lighting.

[47] Eliot, T. S. "Little Gidding." *Four Quartets.* New York: Harcourt, Brace, 1943.

[48] Suzuki, Shunryu, and Trudy Dixon. *Zen Mind, Beginner's Mind.* New York: Walker/Weatherhill, 1970. Print.